MathFlare

Name: ______________________

Class: ___________

Teacher: _______________________

Introduction

As parents and educators, we recognize the pivotal role mathematics plays in shaping a child's academic journey and future success. Yet, the path to mathematical proficiency can often seem daunting, fraught with challenges and complexities. That's where the transformative power of MathFlare Workbooks shine through, illuminating the way forward with clarity, precision, and purpose.

Introducing MathFlare Workbooks – a beacon of guidance, a testament to excellence, and a catalyst for achievement. Crafted with meticulous care and expertise, MathFlare Workbooks stand as paragons of educational excellence, designed to nurture young minds, ignite a passion for learning, and develop a deep-rooted understanding of mathematical concepts.

Picture this: your child eagerly delves into the pages of Mathflare Workbook, greeted by a step-by-step guide illuminated with vivid examples that demystify complex mathematical concepts. With each turn of the page, they embark on a journey of discovery, encountering thoughtfully curated practice questions that reinforce learning and hone problem-solving skills. And when they unveil the answers to those very questions, a sense of accomplishment blossoms within them – a tangible reward for their hard work and dedication.

But MathFlare Workbooks are more than just tools for learning; they are pathways to comprehension, fostering a deep-seated understanding of mathematical concepts through a sequential, logical flow. From fundamental principles to advanced problem-solving strategies, every chapter builds upon the last, ensuring a robust foundation upon which future knowledge can be constructed.

As parents, we yearn for nothing more than to see our children thrive, to witness the spark of inspiration ignited within them as they conquer academic challenges with confidence and poise. MathFlare Workbooks serve as partners in this noble endeavor, offering not just practice questions, but the keys to unlocking a world of opportunity.

And for teachers, MathFlare Workbooks stand as invaluable allies in the quest to cultivate mathematical proficiency in the classroom. With answers readily available, instructors can focus on guiding and nurturing their students, confident in the knowledge that MathFlare Workbooks provide a solid framework upon which to build.

In the pages of MathFlare Workbooks, we find not just the promise of academic excellence, but the seeds of a brighter tomorrow. So let us embrace the power of mathematics, let us champion the journey of learning, and let us pave the way for a generation of young minds poised to shape the world. With MathFlare Workbooks as our guide, the possibilities are infinite, and the future, bright.

Table of Contents

Long Division	
Long Division	1
Long Division: Remainders	28

MathFlare
Grade 2
MATH WORKBOOK
Step by Step Guide and Essential Practice with Answers
Addition Subtraction
Multiplication
Place Value and Expanded Notations
Geometry
MathFlare Publishing

MathFlare
Grade 2-3
MATH WORKBOOK
Step by Step Guide and Essential Practice with Answers
Addition Subtraction
Multiplication and Division
Place Value and Expanded Notations
Geometry
MathFlare Publishing

MathFlare
Grade 3
MATH WORKBOOK
Step by Step Guide and Essential Practice with Answers
Multiplication and Division
Decimals
Place Value and Expanded Notations
Fractions and Geometry
MathFlare Publishing

MathFlare
Grade 1
MATH WORKBOOK
Step by Step Guide and Essential Practice with Answers
Counting and Numbers
Addition and Subtraction
Place Value and Expanded Notations
Understanding Time
MathFlare Publishing

MathFlare
Grade 1-2
MATH WORKBOOK
Step by Step Guide and Essential Practice with Answers
Counting and Numbers
Addition and Subtraction
Place Value and Expanded Notations
Understanding Time
MathFlare Publishing

MathFlare
Grade 3-4
MATH WORKBOOK
Step by Step Guide and Essential Practice with Answers
Addition Subtraction
Multiplication Division
Place Value and Expanded Notations
Fractions and Geometry
MathFlare Publishing

MathFlare
Grade 4
MATH WORKBOOK
Step by Step Guide and Essential Practice with Answers
Addition Subtraction
Multiplication Division
Place Value and Expanded Notations
Fractions and Geometry
MathFlare Publishing

MathFlare
Grade 4-5
MATH WORKBOOK
Step by Step Guide and Essential Practice with Answers
Multiplication Division
Place Value and Expanded Notations
Fractions and Geometry
Unit Conversion
MathFlare Publishing

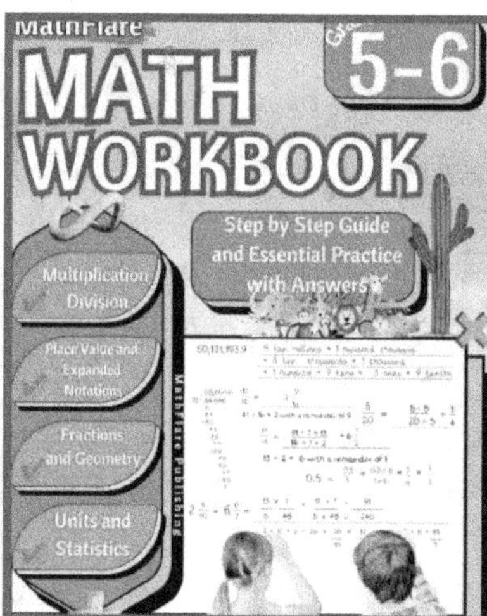

Long Division

Long Division and Remainders

Division is like the opposite of multiplication. It's all about sharing or distributing items equally among a certain number of groups or people.

When we divide one number by another, we're essentially splitting a number into equal parts. We're figuring out how many groups of a certain size can be made from that number.

For instance, let's divide 20 by 4.

When we divide 20 by 4, we're essentially asking, "How many groups of size 4 can we make from 20?"

Now, there are several parts or terms involved in the division process:

- **Dividend:** This is the number being divided, which in this case, is 20.

- **Divisor:** This is the number we're dividing by, which is 4.

- **Quotient:** This is the answer we get after dividing. It tells us how many groups of divisors can be made from the dividend. In this case, the answer is 5.

- **Remainder:** when the divisor doesn't evenly divide the dividend, we get the remainder.

So, when we divide 20 by 4, we found out that 5 groups of 4 can be made from 20.

Let's solve problems from exercises:

```
      4              42              477
   4)16          12)504          6)2,862
    -16            -48             -24
      0             24              46
                   -24            -42
                     0             42
                                  -42
                                    0


       8,965 R1            08,464.6
    9)80,686           10)84,646
     -72                   -0
      86                   84
     -81                  -80
      58                   46
     -54                  -40
      46                   64
     -45                  -60
       1                   46
                          -40
                           60
                          -60
                            0
```

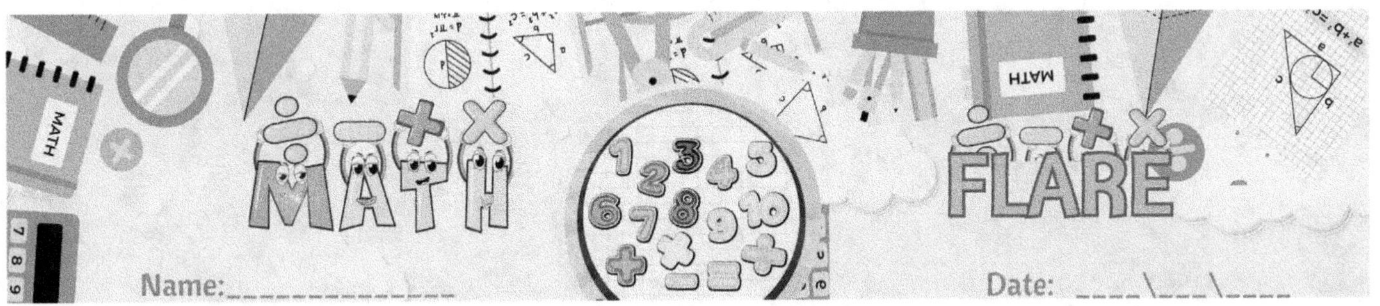

Long Division

Find the quotient.

1.
$4\overline{)196}$

2.
$8\overline{)144}$

3.
$12\overline{)1,104}$

4.
$6\overline{)228}$

5.
$9\overline{)585}$

6.
$2\overline{)8}$

7.
$5\overline{)130}$

8.
$8\overline{)696}$

9.
$3\overline{)225}$

10.
$8\overline{)544}$

11.
$12\overline{)192}$

12.
$5\overline{)400}$

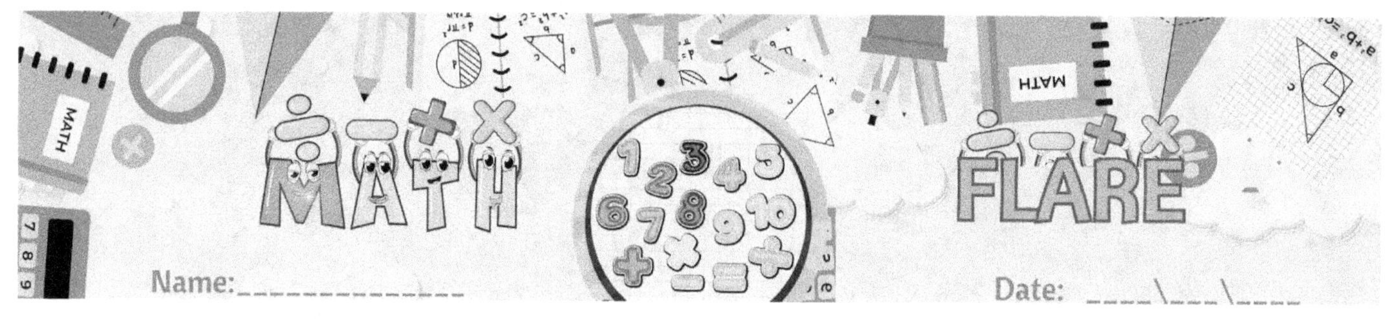

13. 8)̄336

14. 12)̄600

15. 10)̄80

16. 2)̄64

17. 6)̄594

18. 10)̄800

19. 3)̄243

20. 5)̄145

21. 8)̄680

22. 2)̄32

23. 4)̄112

24. 4)̄92

25. 8)̄552

26. 11)̄154

27. 4)̄44

28. 3)̄261

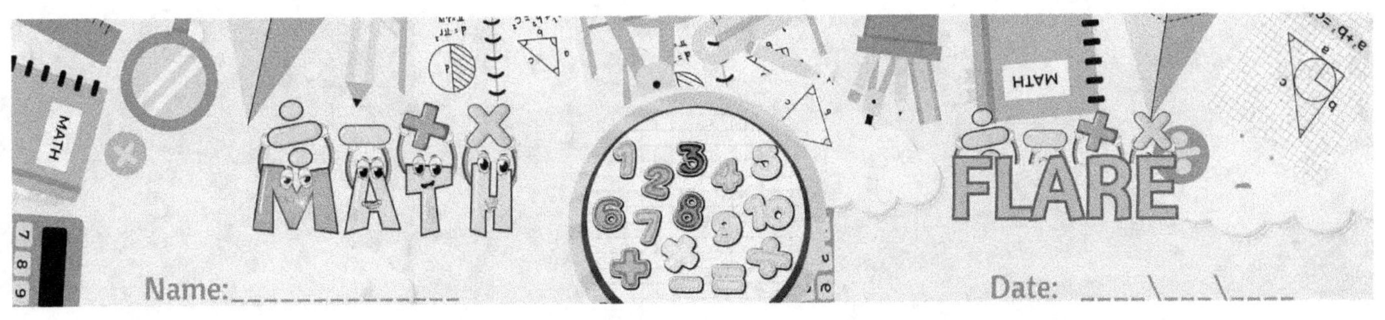

29.

6)‾342

30.

11)‾1,034

31.

7)‾448

32.

7)‾560

33.

7)‾266

34.

5)‾440

35.

9)‾351

36.

5)‾190

37.

1)‾14

38.

2)‾36

39.

7)‾294

40.

10)‾560

41.

4)‾228

42.

6)‾270

43.

5)‾180

44.

9)‾675

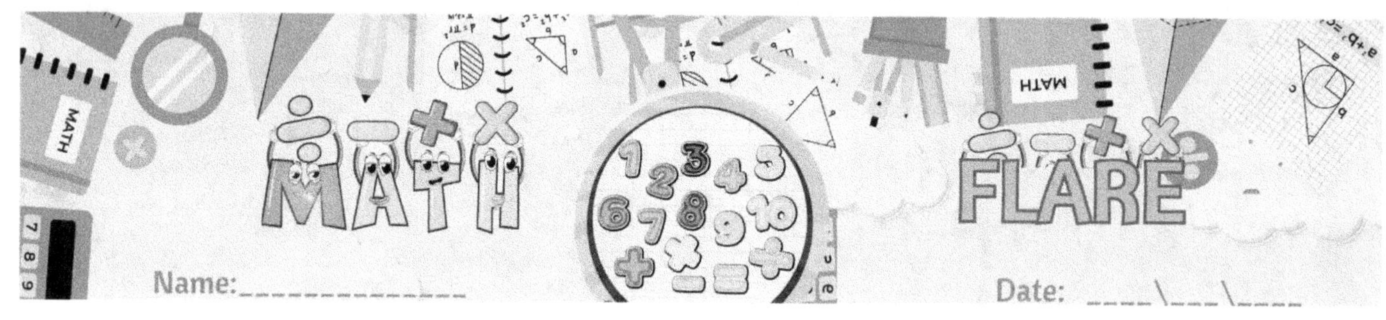

45. $8\overline{)224}$

46. $4\overline{)308}$

47. $5\overline{)360}$

48. $4\overline{)184}$

49. $8\overline{)392}$

50. $9\overline{)216}$

51. $1\overline{)37}$

52. $6\overline{)156}$

53. $2\overline{)34}$

54. $1\overline{)99}$

55. $5\overline{)45}$

56. $9\overline{)27}$

57. $3\overline{)24}$

58. $6\overline{)120}$

59. $8\overline{)520}$

60. $2\overline{)128}$

61. $1\overline{)31}$

62. $11\overline{)671}$

63. $7\overline{)35}$

64. $9\overline{)522}$

65. $7\overline{)616}$

66. $3\overline{)246}$

67. $4\overline{)216}$

68. $9\overline{)594}$

69. $11\overline{)264}$

70. $1\overline{)95}$

71. $1\overline{)24}$

72. $2\overline{)108}$

73. $7\overline{)259}$

74. $2\overline{)10}$

75. $3\overline{)195}$

76. $4\overline{)176}$

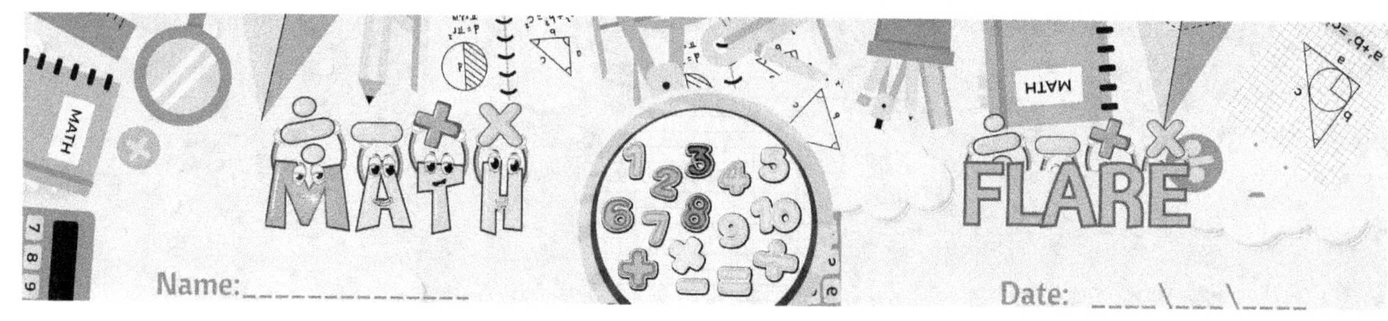

77. $6\overline{)186}$

78. $5\overline{)95}$

79. $10\overline{)810}$

80. $11\overline{)44}$

81. $11\overline{)660}$

82. $11\overline{)165}$

83. $11\overline{)638}$

84. $7\overline{)581}$

85. $8\overline{)72}$

86. $4\overline{)256}$

87. $5\overline{)490}$

88. $1\overline{)19}$

89. $9\overline{)36}$

90. $12\overline{)636}$

91. $3\overline{)189}$

92. $10\overline{)830}$

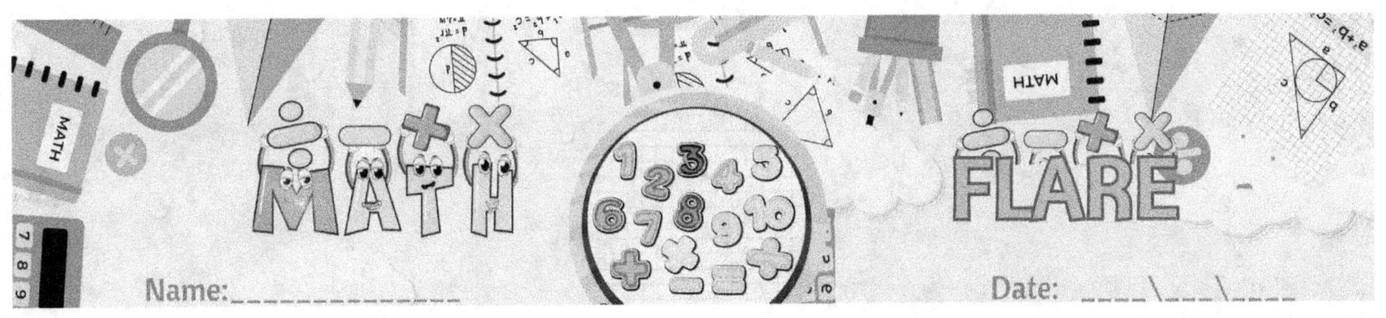

93.

$$2\overline{)44}$$

94.

$$8\overline{)376}$$

95.

$$7\overline{)301}$$

96.

$$6\overline{)336}$$

97.

$$7\overline{)252}$$

98.

$$1\overline{)47}$$

99.

$$7\overline{)462}$$

100.

$$2\overline{)96}$$

101.

$$5\overline{)125}$$

102.

$$3\overline{)198}$$

103.

$$2\overline{)184}$$

104.

$$1\overline{)39}$$

105.

$$5\overline{)260}$$

106.

$$11\overline{)737}$$

107.

$$5\overline{)455}$$

108.

$$12\overline{)948}$$

109. 12)‾84

110. 5)‾65

111. 7)‾413

112. 9)‾180

113. 6)‾492

114. 3)‾222

115. 4)‾240

116. 3)‾111

117. 3)‾84

118. 7)‾539

119. 3)‾183

120. 7)‾322

121. 4)‾388

122. 8)‾472

123. 11)‾946

124. 5)‾205

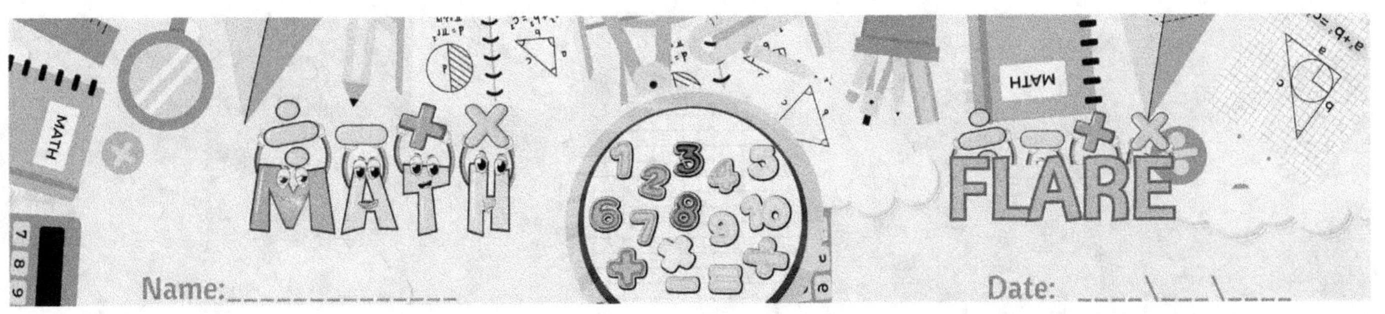

125.

11)561

126.

8)264

127.

6)384

128.

8)320

129.

2)100

130.

11)1,089

131.

11)55

132.

5)250

133.

2)198

134.

1)92

135.

4)104

136.

4)188

137.

4)88

138.

7)343

139.

11)99

140.

7)210

141.

$5 \overline{)320}$

142.

$6 \overline{)126}$

143.

$4 \overline{)220}$

144.

$12 \overline{)1,164}$

145.

$2 \overline{)2}$

146.

$7 \overline{)231}$

147.

$1 \overline{)12}$

148.

$6 \overline{)114}$

149.

$7 \overline{)644}$

150.

$10 \overline{)480}$

151.

$3 \overline{)42}$

152.

$2 \overline{)54}$

153.

$2 \overline{)28}$

154.

$6 \overline{)36}$

155.

$11 \overline{)682}$

156.

$1 \overline{)15}$

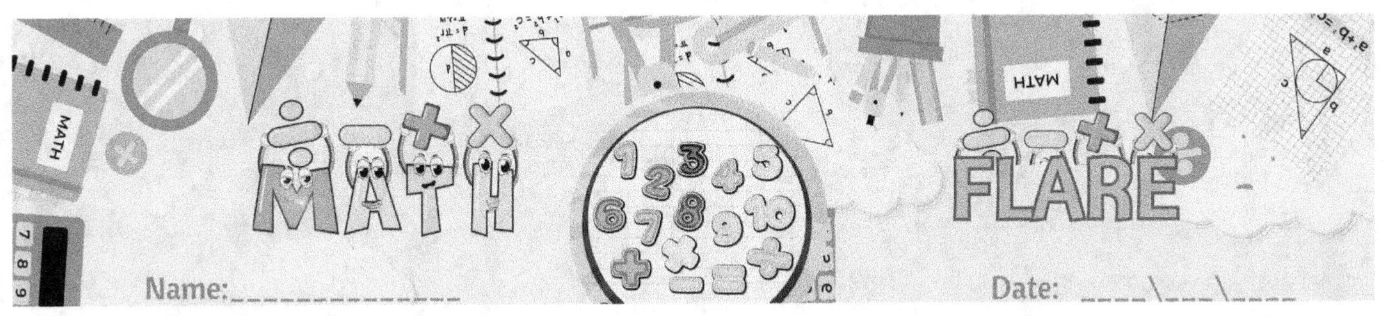

157.

$8 \overline{)592}$

158.

$1 \overline{)87}$

159.

$9 \overline{)432}$

160.

$11 \overline{)341}$

161.

$3 \overline{)96}$

162.

$3 \overline{)144}$

163.

$1 \overline{)73}$

164.

$7 \overline{)455}$

165.

$6 \overline{)294}$

166.

$8 \overline{)600}$

167.

$6 \overline{)210}$

168.

$3 \overline{)9}$

169.

$6 \overline{)516}$

170.

$6 \overline{)42}$

171.

$2 \overline{)188}$

172.

$4 \overline{)360}$

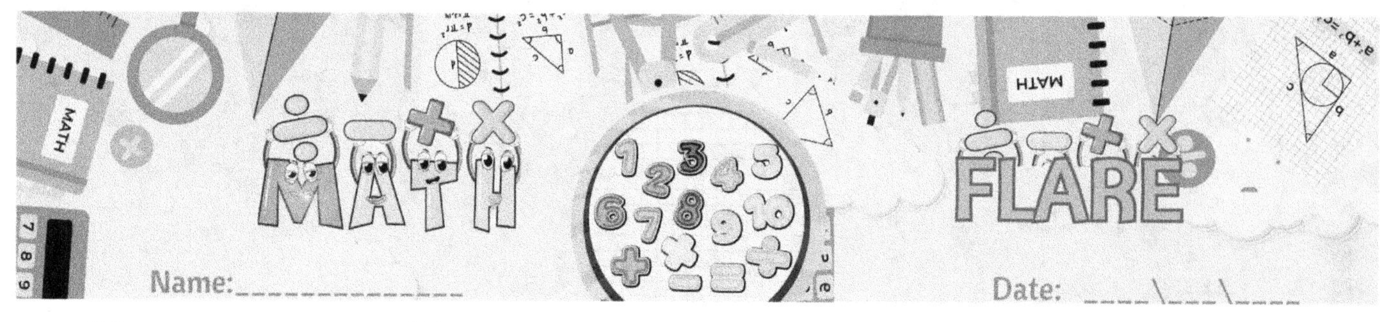

173.

6)426

174.

3)192

175.

3)114

176.

6)522

177.

3)36

178.

2)116

179.

2)150

180.

6)180

181.

3)159

182.

6)546

183.

4)272

184.

9)612

185.

12)96

186.

4)392

187.

8)232

188.

1)35

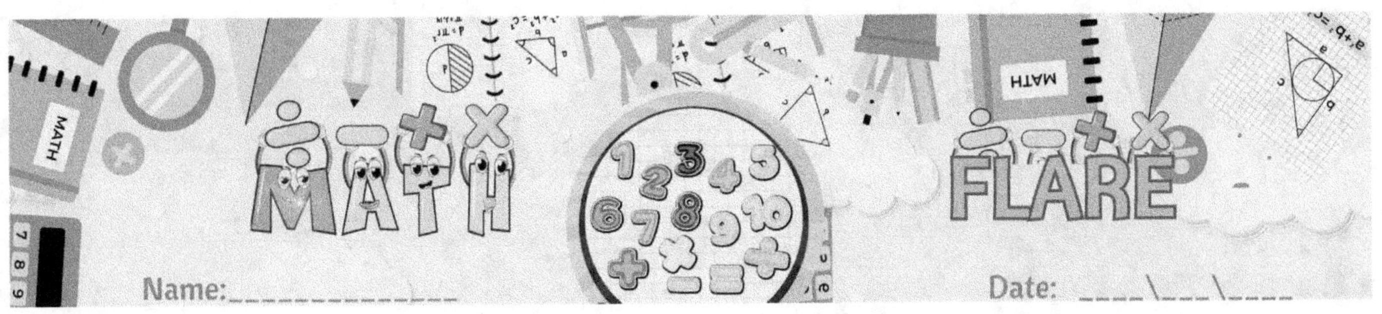

189.

$7\overline{)651}$

190.

$6\overline{)48}$

191.

$11\overline{)913}$

192.

$4\overline{)232}$

193.

$11\overline{)1,012}$

194.

$10\overline{)740}$

195.

$9\overline{)702}$

196.

$5\overline{)275}$

197.

$6\overline{)300}$

198.

$11\overline{)605}$

199.

$5\overline{)245}$

200.

$1\overline{)43}$

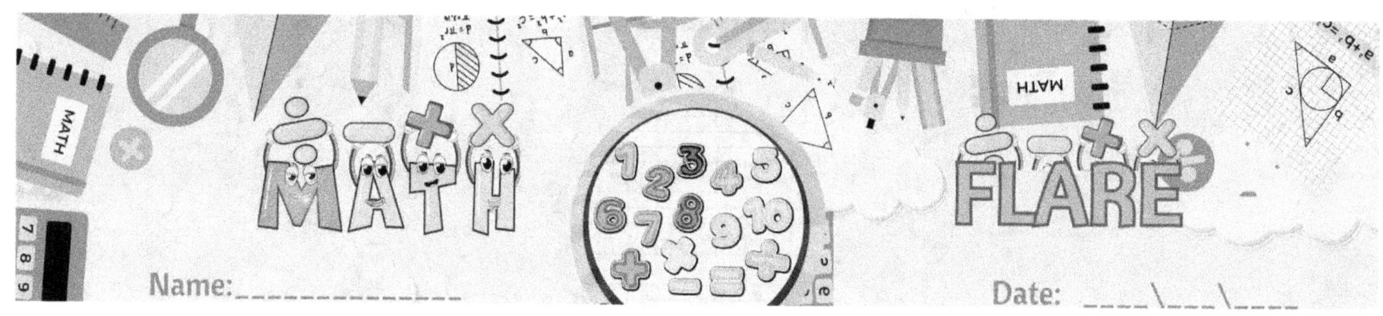

Long Division

Find the quotient.

1.

$13\overline{)3,081}$

2.

$10\overline{)8,120}$

3.

$11\overline{)8,151}$

4.

$5\overline{)2,790}$

5.

$18\overline{)1,656}$

6.

$12\overline{)7,992}$

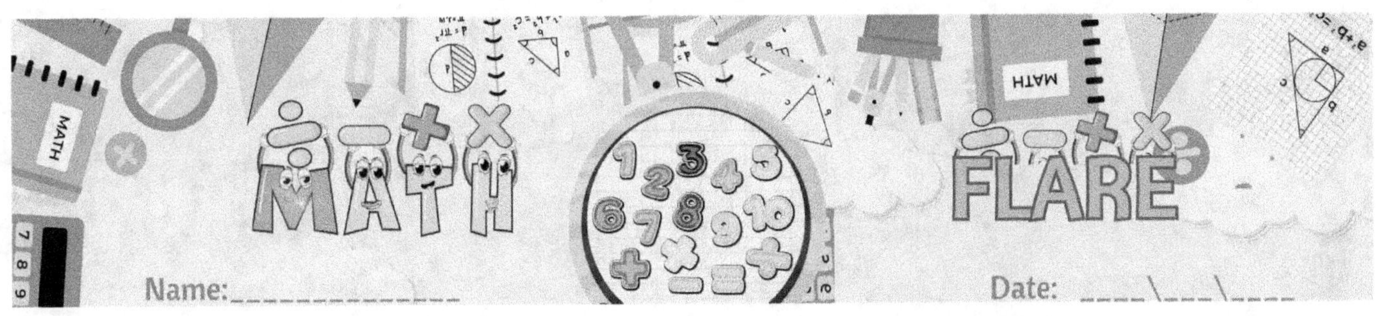

7.

$$13\overline{)9{,}191}$$

8.

$$11\overline{)7{,}634}$$

9.

$$15\overline{)930}$$

10.

$$6\overline{)504}$$

11.

$$10\overline{)4{,}860}$$

12.

$$5\overline{)4{,}275}$$

13.

$$18\overline{)8{,}802}$$

14.

$$19\overline{)1{,}425}$$

15.

$$1\overline{)876}$$

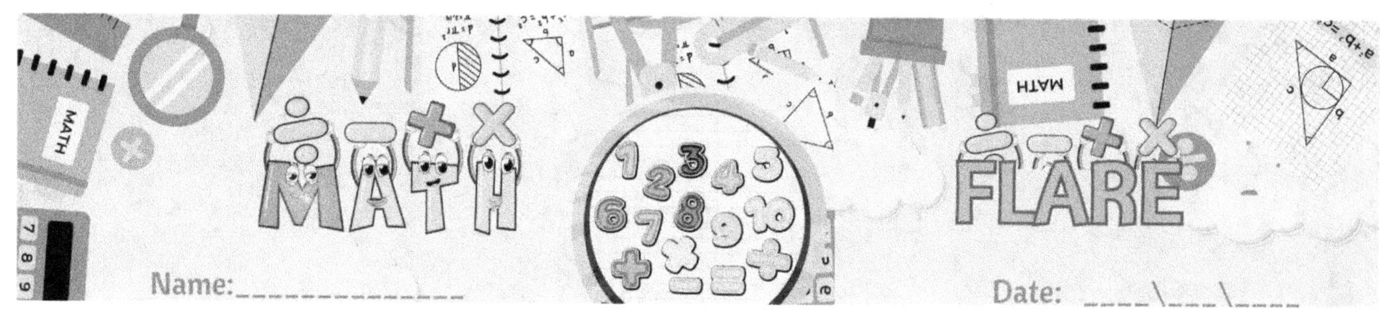

16.

$14 \overline{)6,412}$

17.

$16 \overline{)13,280}$

18.

$19 \overline{)16,986}$

19.

$12 \overline{)1,416}$

20.

$8 \overline{)304}$

21.

$11 \overline{)242}$

22.

$18 \overline{)12,258}$

23.

$5 \overline{)3,690}$

24.

$18 \overline{)12,780}$

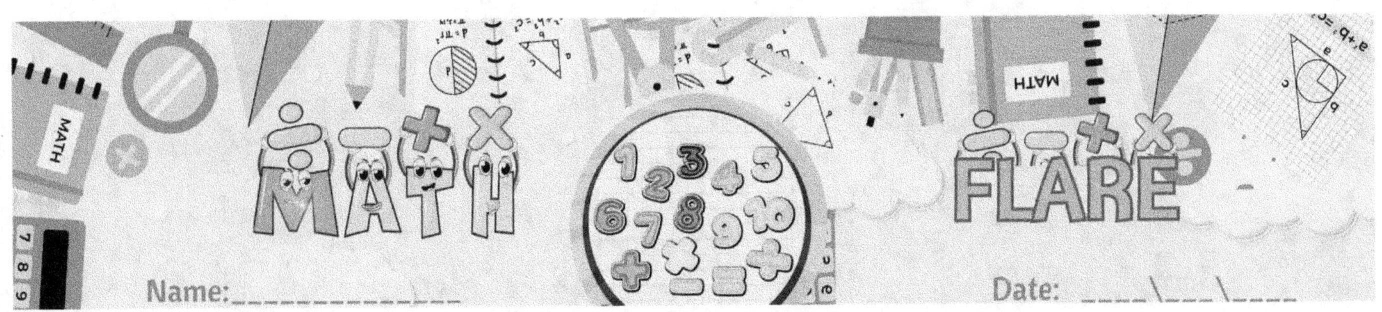

25.

$19\overline{)4{,}104}$

26.

$16\overline{)5{,}376}$

27.

$5\overline{)4{,}650}$

28.

$19\overline{)2{,}584}$

29.

$2\overline{)1{,}242}$

30.

$19\overline{)1{,}045}$

31.

$17\overline{)1{,}921}$

32.

$11\overline{)10{,}967}$

33.

$9\overline{)1{,}179}$

34.

$$17\overline{)13{,}957}$$

35.

$$15\overline{)9{,}675}$$

36.

$$4\overline{)2{,}508}$$

37.

$$14\overline{)3{,}528}$$

38.

$$11\overline{)5{,}203}$$

39.

$$12\overline{)6{,}288}$$

40.

$$14\overline{)1{,}918}$$

41.

$$12\overline{)2{,}580}$$

42.

$$3\overline{)2{,}400}$$

43.

$2 \overline{)684}$

44.

$6 \overline{)5{,}268}$

45.

$18 \overline{)14{,}796}$

46.

$17 \overline{)15{,}912}$

47.

$4 \overline{)1{,}288}$

48.

$5 \overline{)2{,}170}$

49.

$10 \overline{)8{,}930}$

50.

$6 \overline{)372}$

51.

$18 \overline{)1{,}224}$

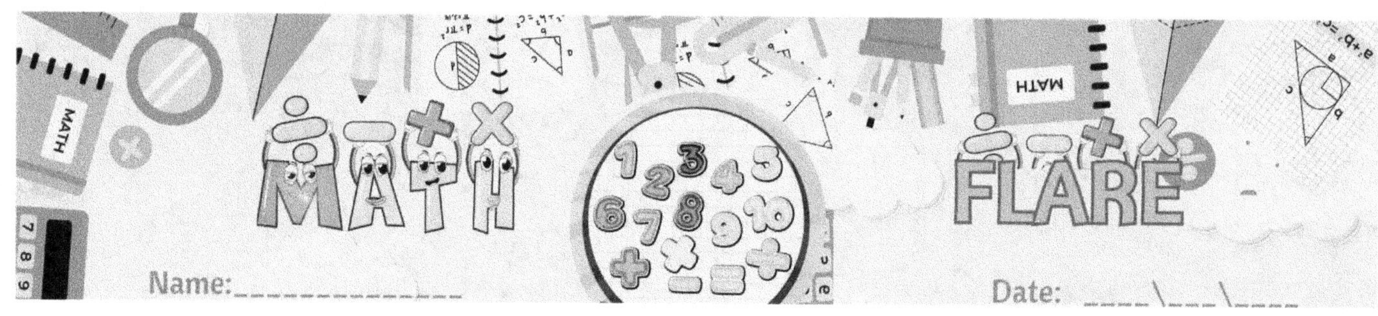

52.

19)5,814

53.

2)348

54.

13)12,259

55.

8)3,640

56.

11)5,577

57.

19)15,200

58.

10)6,030

59.

20)14,800

60.

19)1,387

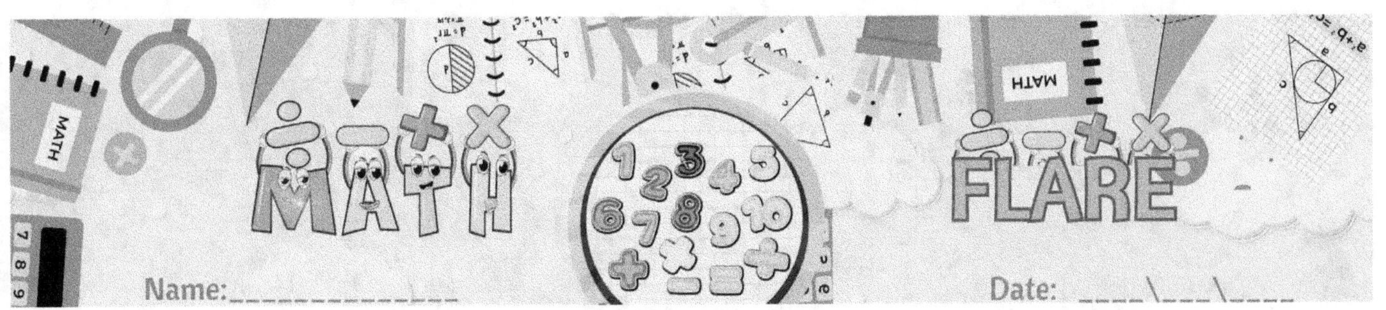

61.

17 ⟌ 16,609

62.

18 ⟌ 16,650

63.

16 ⟌ 3,216

64.

10 ⟌ 3,640

65.

2 ⟌ 206

66.

20 ⟌ 13,980

67.

6 ⟌ 3,618

68.

6 ⟌ 3,198

69.

6 ⟌ 4,896

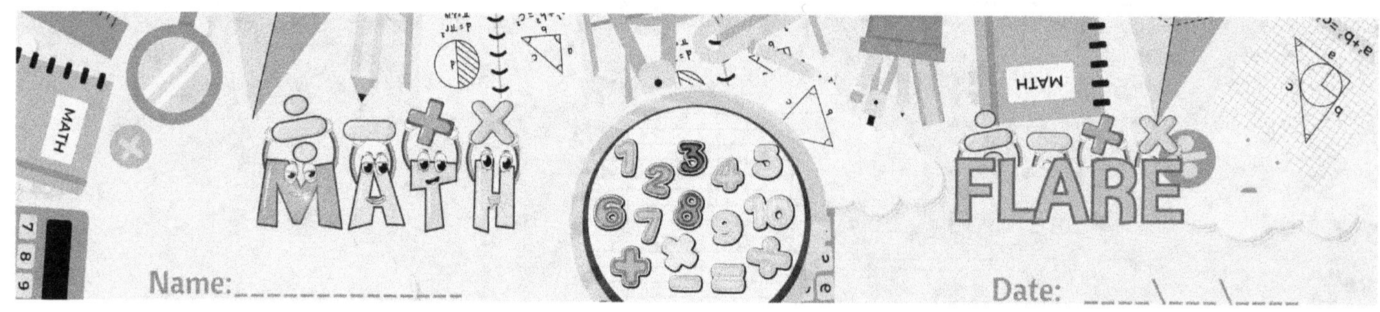

70.

$$15\overline{)13{,}530}$$

71.

$$14\overline{)4{,}452}$$

72.

$$10\overline{)4{,}470}$$

73.

$$6\overline{)2{,}142}$$

74.

$$20\overline{)7{,}580}$$

75.

$$17\overline{)10{,}472}$$

76.

$$9\overline{)6{,}651}$$

77.

$$19\overline{)3{,}724}$$

78.

$$5\overline{)4{,}515}$$

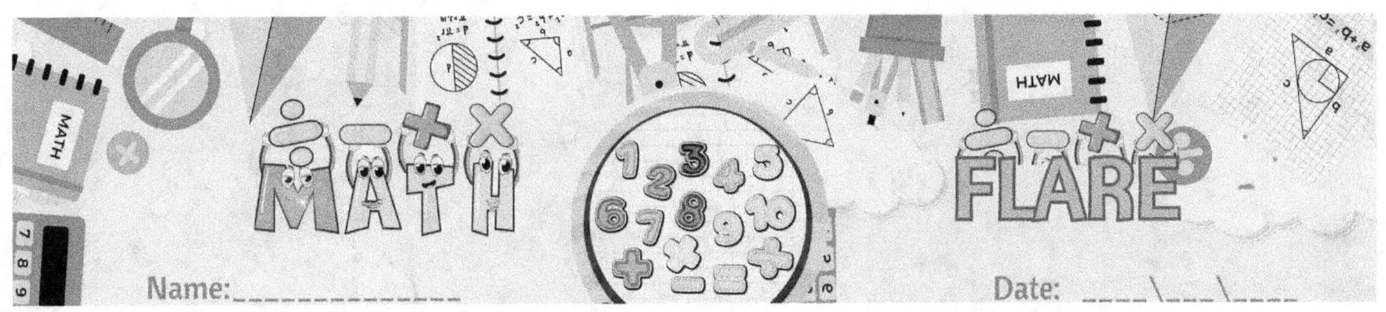

79.

$$4 \overline{)144}$$

80.

$$11 \overline{)9{,}647}$$

81.

$$15 \overline{)4{,}290}$$

82.

$$18 \overline{)5{,}238}$$

83.

$$10 \overline{)8{,}410}$$

84.

$$6 \overline{)2{,}124}$$

85.

$$11 \overline{)10{,}131}$$

86.

$$8 \overline{)1{,}392}$$

87.

$$1 \overline{)20}$$

88.

$$8\overline{)4,400}$$

89.

$$10\overline{)4,720}$$

90.

$$13\overline{)5,525}$$

91.

$$5\overline{)350}$$

92.

$$10\overline{)4,160}$$

93.

$$14\overline{)3,556}$$

94.

$$9\overline{)3,168}$$

95.

$$8\overline{)1,752}$$

96.

$$7\overline{)5,908}$$

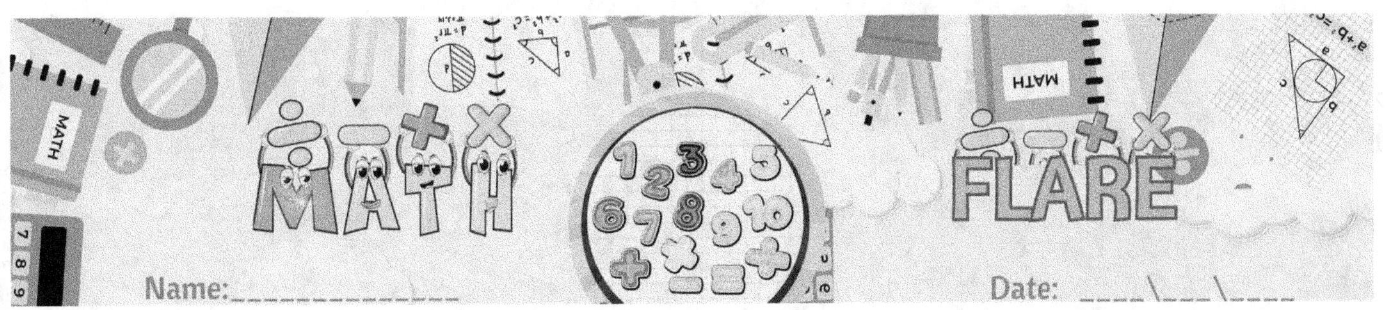

97. $4 \overline{)1{,}624}$

98. $9 \overline{)1{,}755}$

99. $20 \overline{)8{,}820}$

100. $3 \overline{)1{,}875}$

101. $17 \overline{)16{,}065}$

102. $6 \overline{)1{,}632}$

103. $15 \overline{)14{,}295}$

104. $16 \overline{)10{,}272}$

105. $9 \overline{)6{,}093}$

106.

$$8\overline{)800}$$

107.

$$13\overline{)8{,}541}$$

108.

$$16\overline{)7{,}952}$$

109.

$$13\overline{)2{,}730}$$

110.

$$3\overline{)567}$$

111.

$$19\overline{)3{,}705}$$

112.

$$11\overline{)1{,}452}$$

113.

$$18\overline{)3{,}132}$$

114.

$$17\overline{)16{,}558}$$

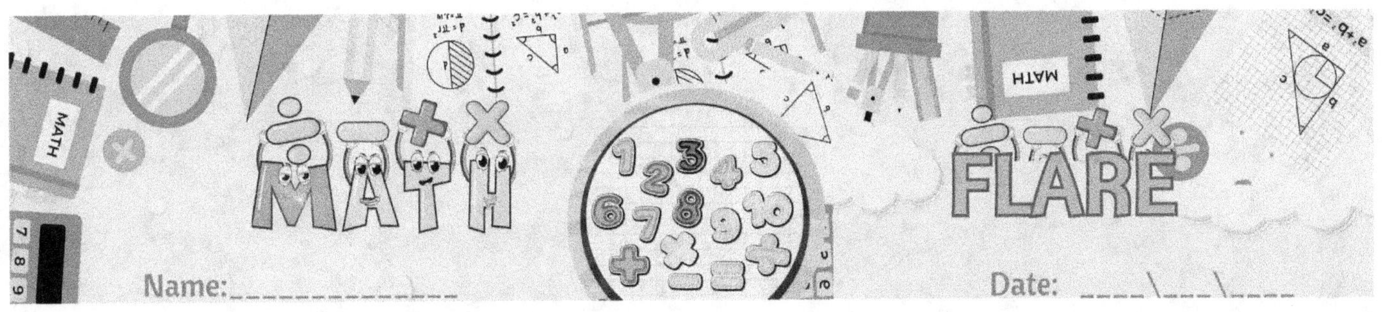

115.

$$4 \overline{)1{,}192}$$

116.

$$10 \overline{)2{,}040}$$

117.

$$7 \overline{)4{,}172}$$

118.

$$5 \overline{)2{,}755}$$

119.

$$4 \overline{)1{,}548}$$

120.

$$11 \overline{)8{,}503}$$

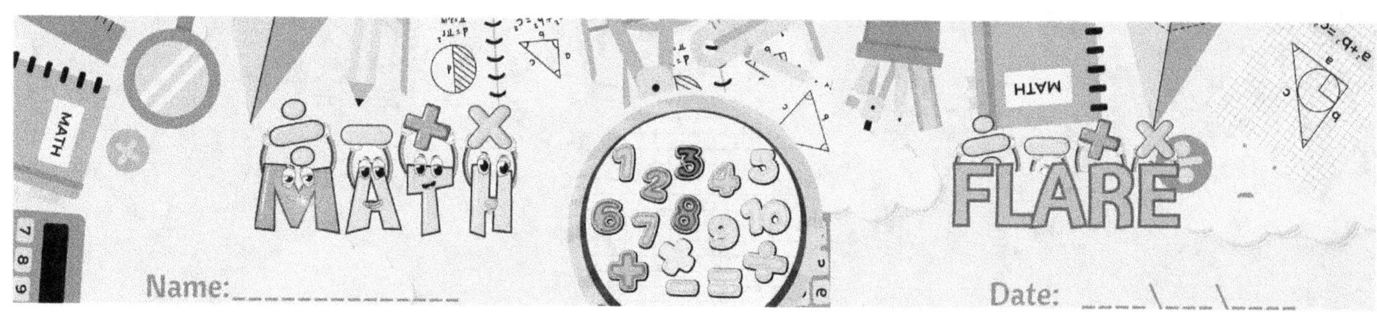

Long Division: Remainders

Find the quotient.

1.

$$16\overline{)32{,}232}$$

2.

$$15\overline{)94{,}651}$$

3.

$$5\overline{)84{,}509}$$

4.

$$11\overline{)26{,}955}$$

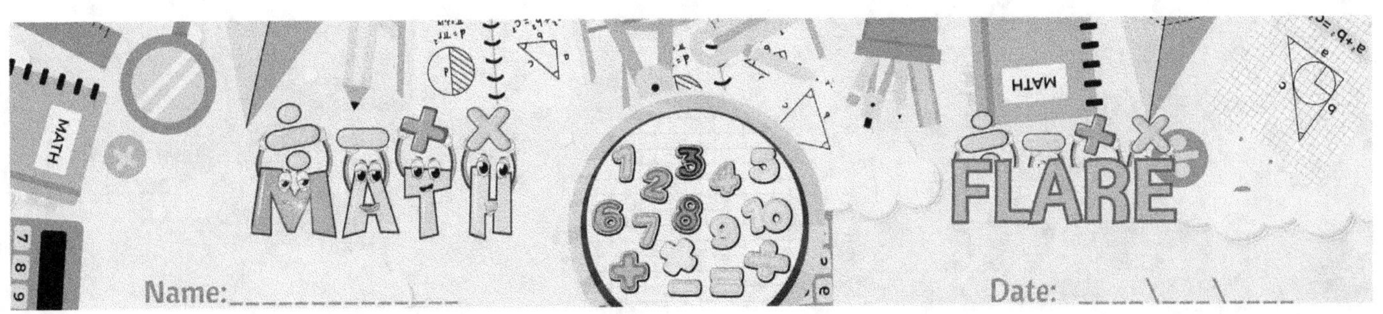

5.

$$18\overline{)65{,}514}$$

6.

$$16\overline{)60{,}552}$$

7.

$$19\overline{)39{,}336}$$

8.

$$13\overline{)71{,}346}$$

9.

$$4\overline{)46{,}719}$$

10.

$$12\overline{)45{,}169}$$

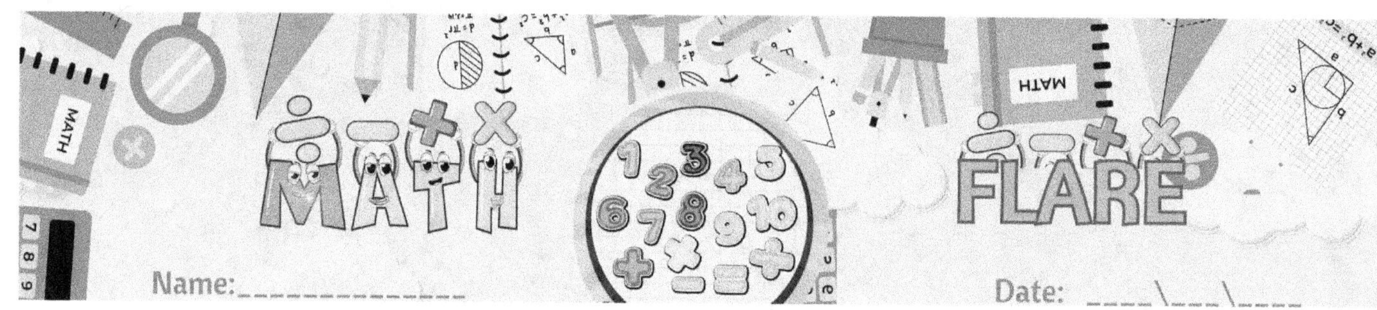

11.

$$17 \overline{) 20{,}104}$$

12.

$$4 \overline{) 54{,}759}$$

13.

$$5 \overline{) 27{,}127}$$

14.

$$3 \overline{) 80{,}257}$$

15.

$$6 \overline{) 47{,}896}$$

16.

$$6 \overline{) 41{,}314}$$

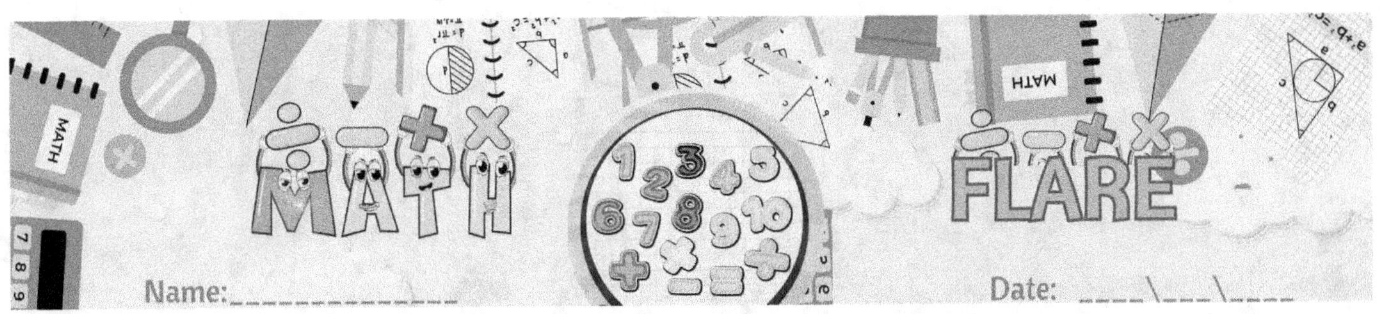

17.

8)71,009

18.

5)94,766

19.

17)32,847

20.

14)37,332

21.

8)98,634

22.

6)42,211

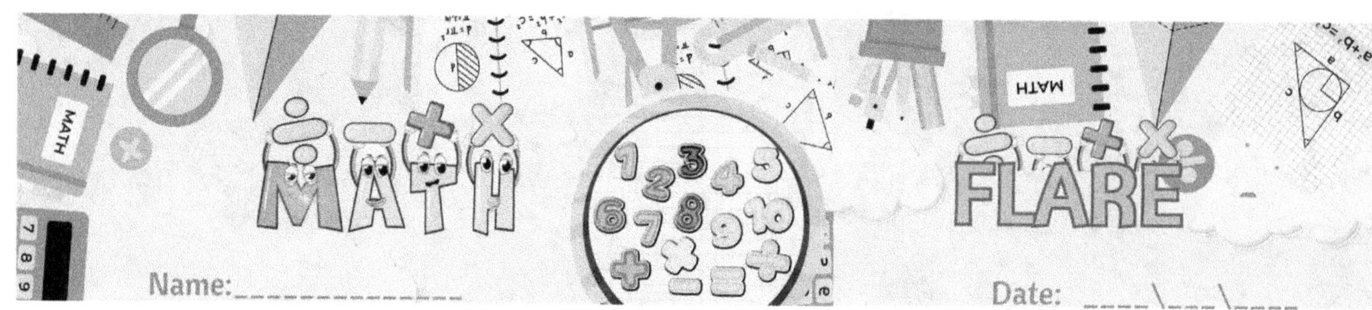

23.

$$15 \overline{)\ 76{,}265}$$

24.

$$9 \overline{)\ 89{,}005}$$

25.

$$13 \overline{)\ 92{,}297}$$

26.

$$2 \overline{)\ 22{,}912}$$

27.

$$20 \overline{)\ 99{,}609}$$

28.

$$9 \overline{)\ 69{,}489}$$

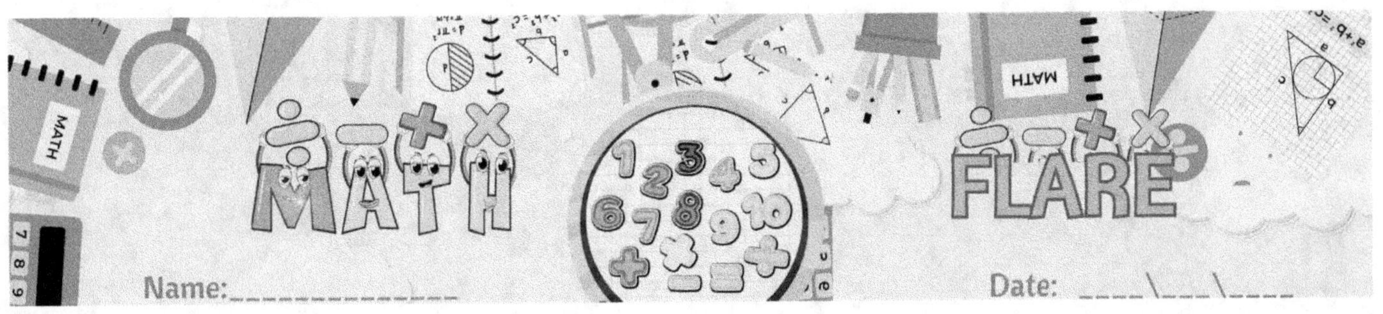

29.

17$\overline{)34,413}$

30.

14$\overline{)56,490}$

31.

4$\overline{)47,100}$

32.

9$\overline{)18,936}$

33.

8$\overline{)60,466}$

34.

20$\overline{)18,817}$

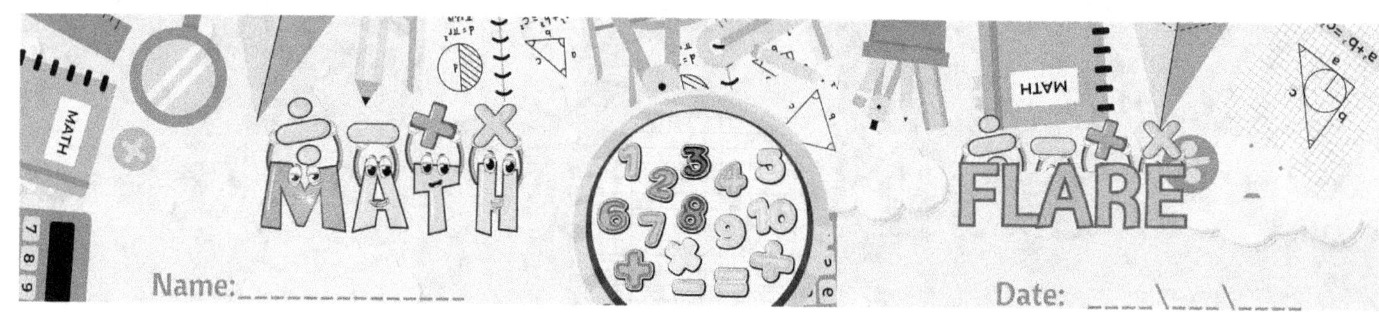

35.

$11 \overline{)97{,}802}$

36.

$12 \overline{)44{,}631}$

37.

$15 \overline{)84{,}811}$

38.

$16 \overline{)60{,}761}$

39.

$7 \overline{)53{,}402}$

40.

$11 \overline{)43{,}922}$

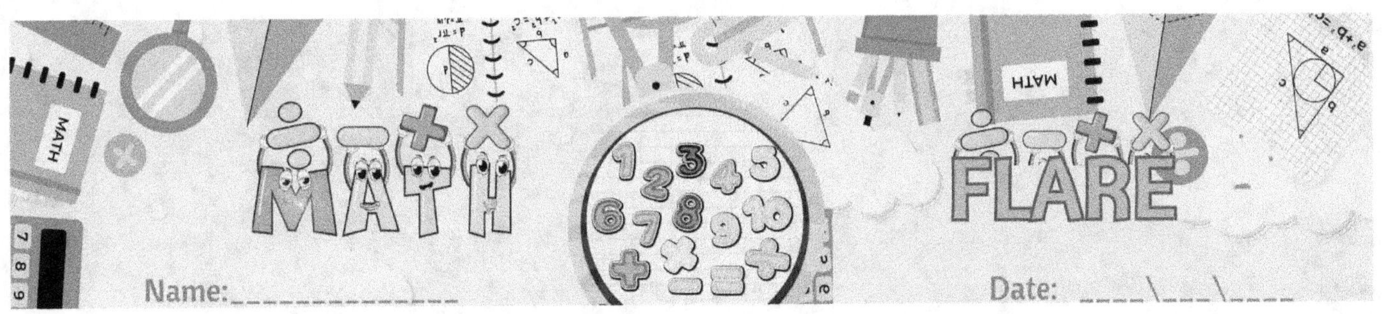

41.

$$9\overline{)37{,}816}$$

42.

$$17\overline{)23{,}147}$$

43.

$$8\overline{)18{,}499}$$

44.

$$15\overline{)32{,}586}$$

45.

$$12\overline{)71{,}247}$$

46.

$$10\overline{)91{,}360}$$

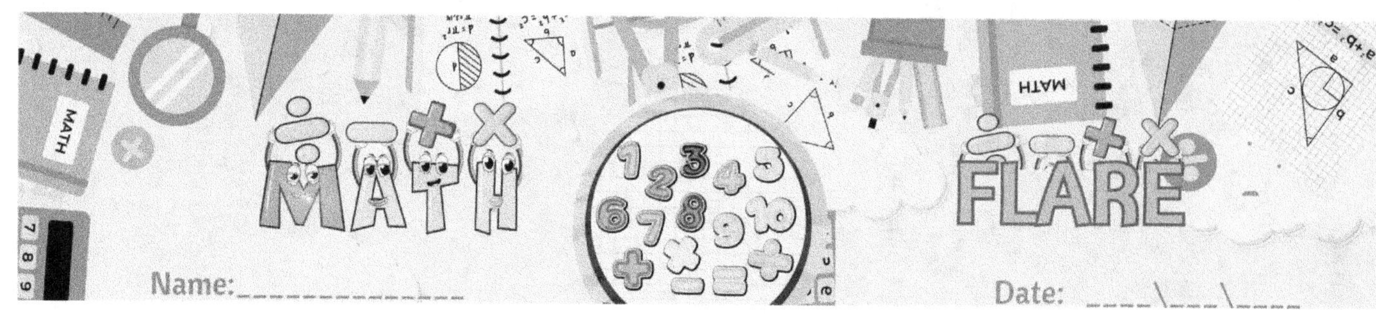

47.

$$14\overline{)38{,}305}$$

48.

$$17\overline{)34{,}840}$$

49.

$$20\overline{)30{,}007}$$

50.

$$10\overline{)70{,}799}$$

51.

$$18\overline{)65{,}197}$$

52.

$$9\overline{)48{,}324}$$

53.

$$12 \overline{)29{,}145}$$

54.

$$7 \overline{)26{,}483}$$

55.

$$18 \overline{)47{,}665}$$

56.

$$2 \overline{)93{,}225}$$

57.

$$3 \overline{)50{,}558}$$

58.

$$3 \overline{)39{,}889}$$

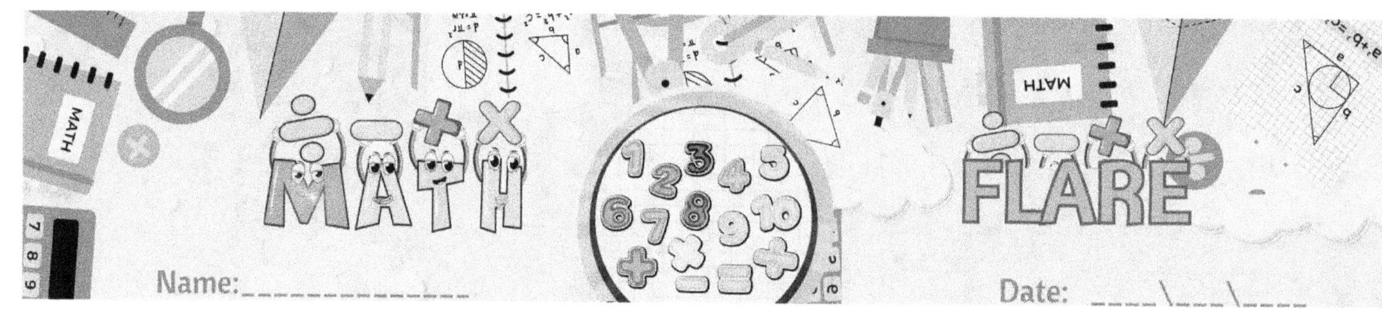

59.

$$7 \overline{)98{,}370}$$

60.

$$6 \overline{)35{,}630}$$

61.

$$9 \overline{)15{,}788}$$

62.

$$10 \overline{)37{,}361}$$

63.

$$19 \overline{)64{,}220}$$

64.

$$5 \overline{)33{,}635}$$

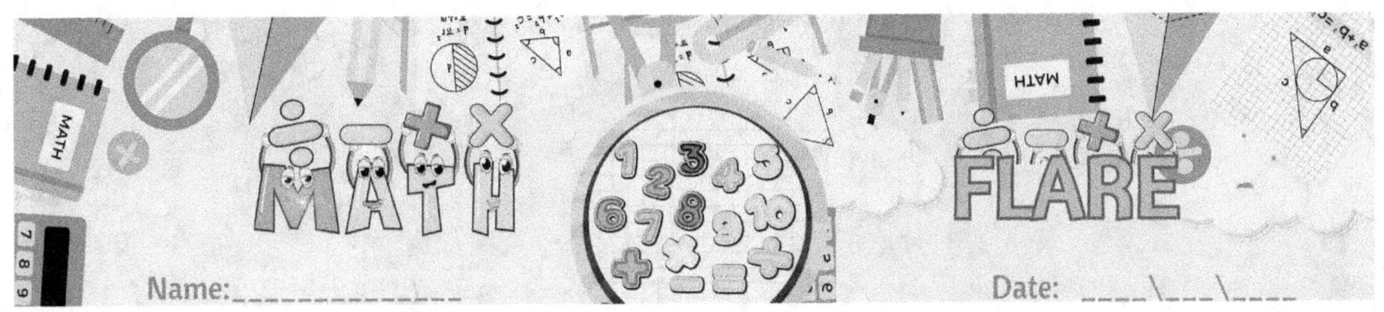

65.

$15 \overline{)48,407}$

66.

$11 \overline{)61,171}$

67.

$19 \overline{)62,701}$

68.

$9 \overline{)87,922}$

69.

$15 \overline{)95,814}$

70.

$12 \overline{)64,992}$

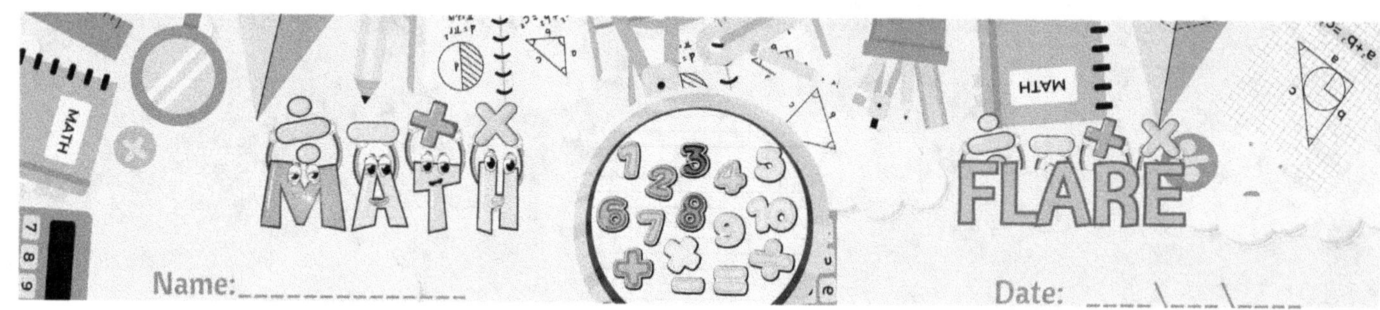

71.

$$19\overline{)23{,}554}$$

72.

$$17\overline{)34{,}934}$$

73.

$$18\overline{)64{,}922}$$

74.

$$7\overline{)97{,}816}$$

75.

$$6\overline{)39{,}756}$$

76.

$$19\overline{)88{,}754}$$

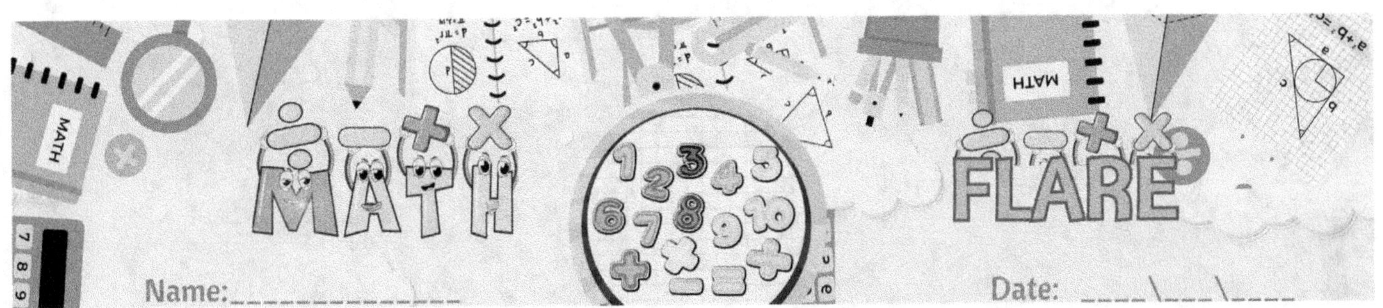

77.

10)72,467

78.

6)42,131

79.

20)63,053

80.

7)82,504

81.

2)37,353

82.

15)87,973

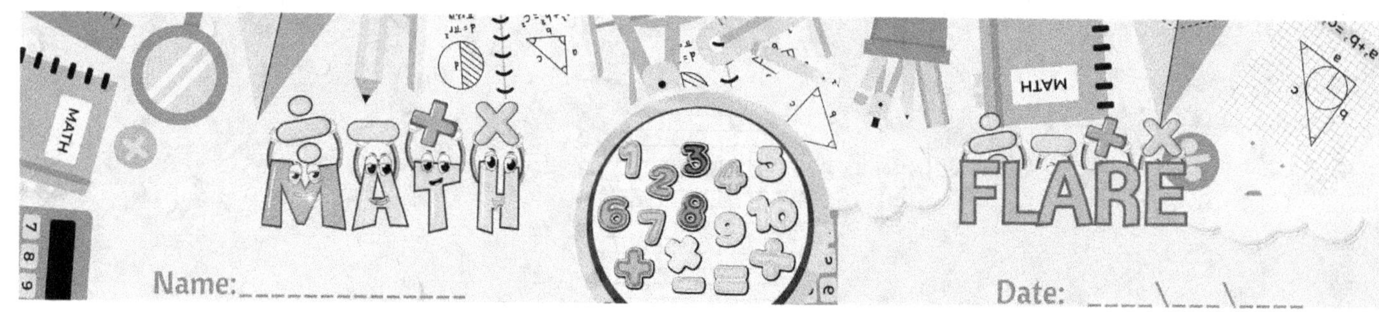

83.

$$10 \overline{)\ 37{,}157}$$

84.

$$11 \overline{)\ 48{,}218}$$

85.

$$18 \overline{)\ 25{,}455}$$

86.

$$6 \overline{)\ 17{,}155}$$

87.

$$16 \overline{)\ 69{,}814}$$

88.

$$4 \overline{)\ 16{,}901}$$

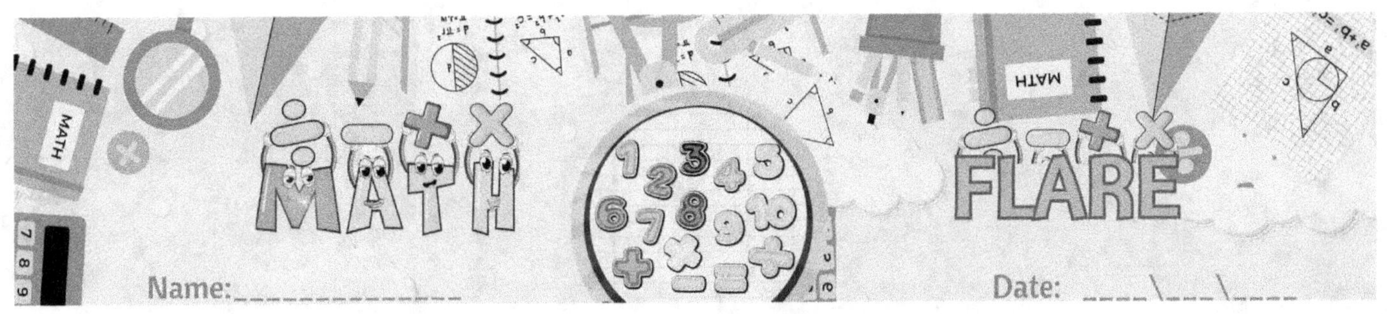

89.

$11 \overline{) 21{,}301}$

90.

$15 \overline{) 84{,}741}$

91.

$20 \overline{) 98{,}439}$

92.

$5 \overline{) 85{,}428}$

93.

$13 \overline{) 84{,}881}$

94.

$4 \overline{) 82{,}844}$

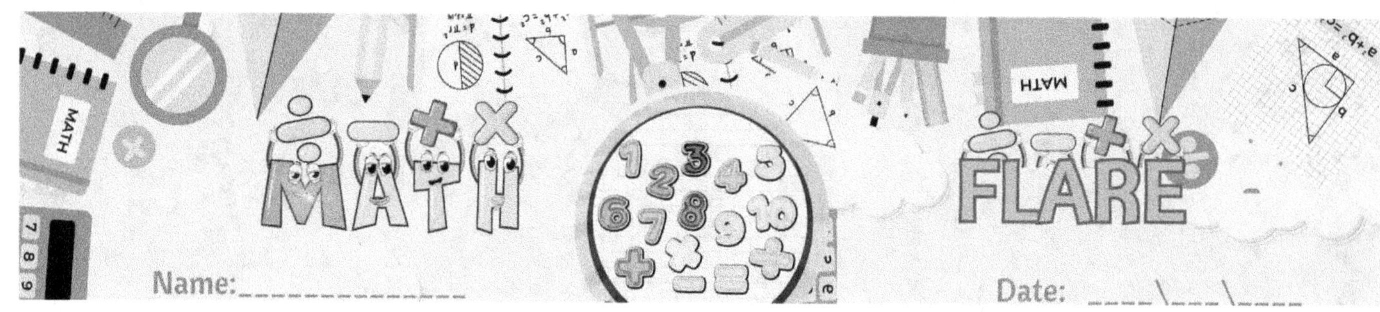

95.

$$14 \overline{)63{,}891}$$

96.

$$19 \overline{)84{,}355}$$

97.

$$8 \overline{)93{,}917}$$

98.

$$4 \overline{)30{,}175}$$

99.

$$12 \overline{)18{,}241}$$

100.

$$5 \overline{)55{,}779}$$

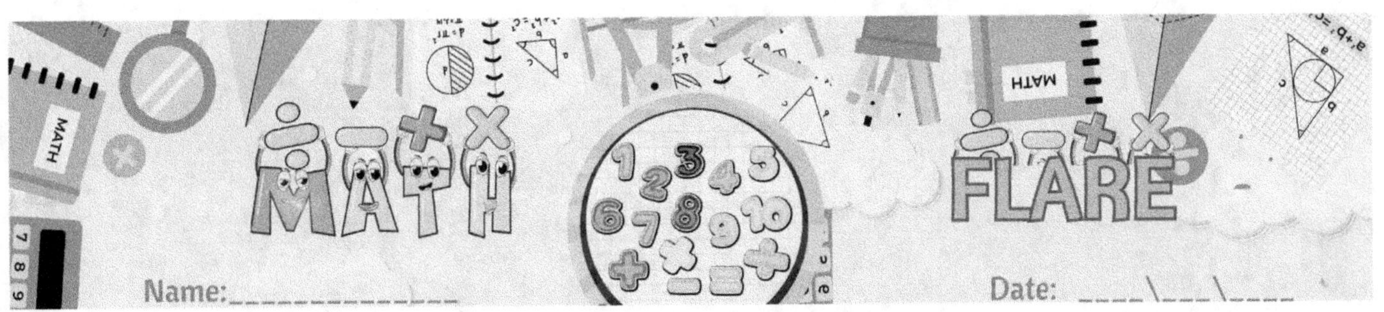

101.

11$\overline{)52{,}240}$

102.

9$\overline{)19{,}490}$

103.

13$\overline{)24{,}733}$

104.

19$\overline{)35{,}394}$

105.

7$\overline{)43{,}469}$

106.

4$\overline{)17{,}688}$

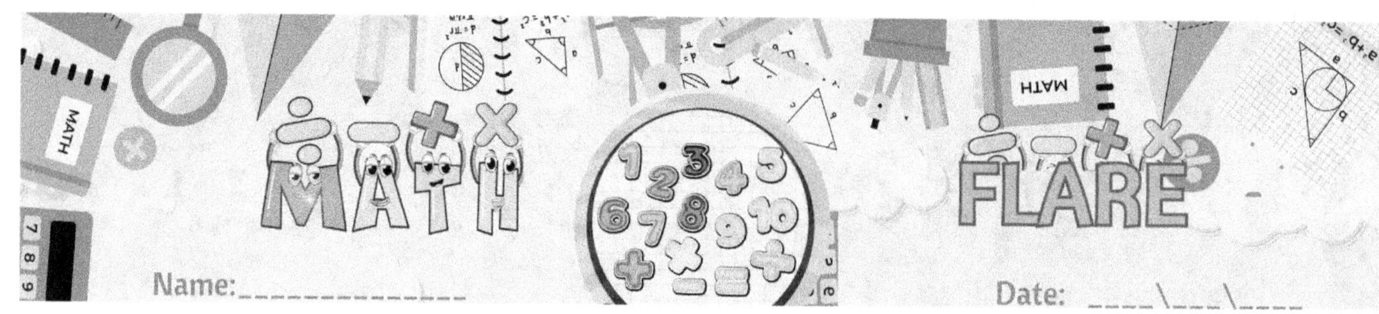

107.

4) 23,927

108.

8) 34,450

109.

14) 25,879

110.

14) 89,147

111.

7) 65,077

112.

11) 90,653

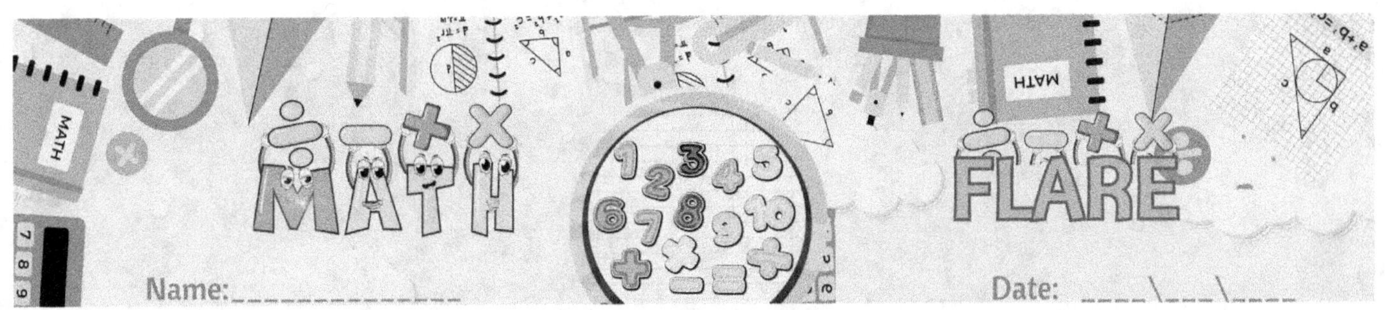

113.

$$4\overline{)18{,}132}$$

114.

$$8\overline{)38{,}041}$$

115.

$$19\overline{)57{,}945}$$

116.

$$12\overline{)11{,}350}$$

117.

$$14\overline{)98{,}653}$$

118.

$$11\overline{)31{,}540}$$

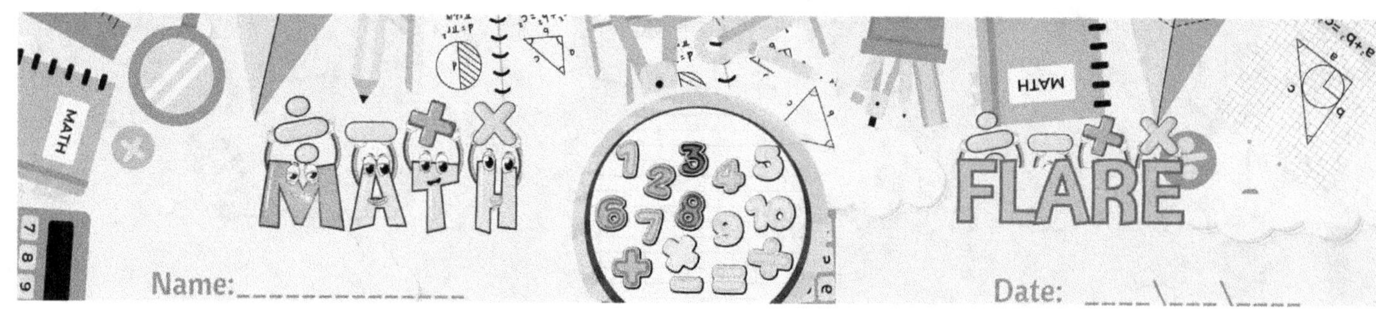

119.

$$10 \overline{)\, 89,218}$$

120.

$$6 \overline{)\, 11,813}$$

121.

$$18 \overline{)\, 40,585}$$

122.

$$8 \overline{)\, 78,878}$$

123.

$$15 \overline{)\, 61,272}$$

124.

$$17 \overline{)\, 83,235}$$

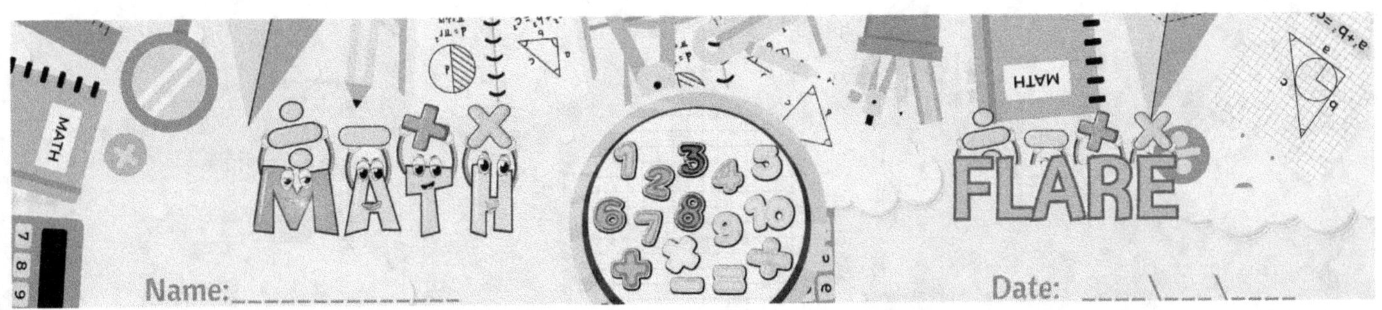

125.

$$18 \overline{)17{,}671}$$

126.

$$9 \overline{)96{,}376}$$

127.

$$17 \overline{)71{,}756}$$

128.

$$5 \overline{)61{,}931}$$

129.

$$13 \overline{)62{,}626}$$

130.

$$3 \overline{)39{,}154}$$

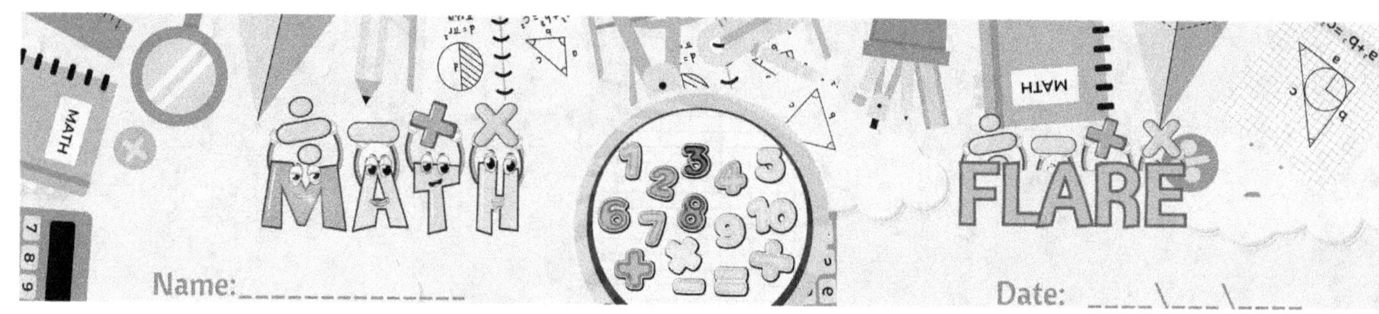

131.

$$20 \overline{)38{,}773}$$

132.

$$10 \overline{)46{,}420}$$

133.

$$11 \overline{)31{,}217}$$

134.

$$11 \overline{)19{,}975}$$

135.

$$16 \overline{)87{,}202}$$

136.

$$16 \overline{)49{,}435}$$

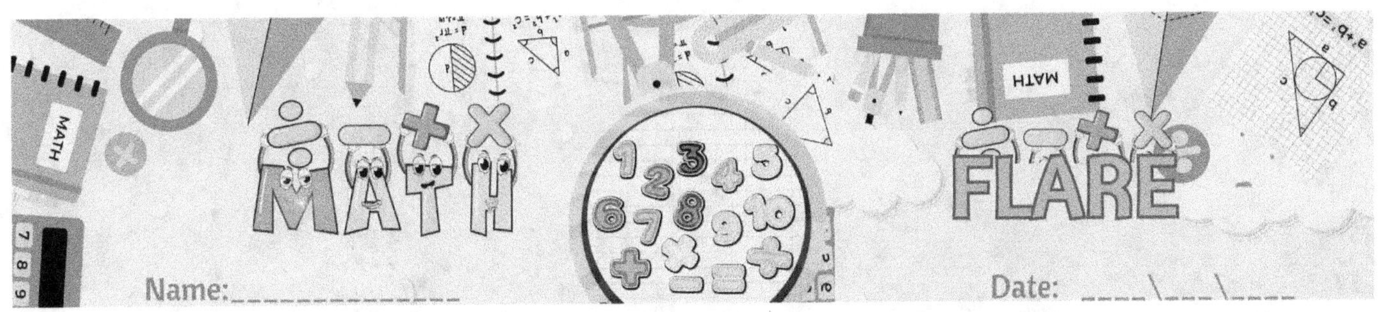

137.

$$14\overline{)69{,}641}$$

138.

$$15\overline{)40{,}609}$$

139.

$$12\overline{)56{,}999}$$

140.

$$8\overline{)95{,}230}$$

141.

$$11\overline{)36{,}765}$$

142.

$$13\overline{)30{,}049}$$

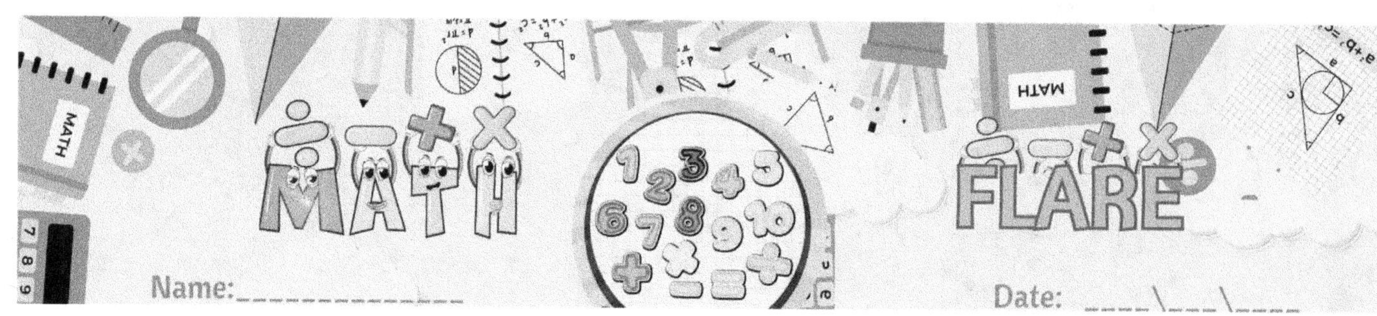

143.

$$13\overline{)98{,}269}$$

144.

$$5\overline{)88{,}639}$$

145.

$$3\overline{)15{,}818}$$

146.

$$7\overline{)92{,}541}$$

147.

$$19\overline{)19{,}016}$$

148.

$$9\overline{)89{,}311}$$

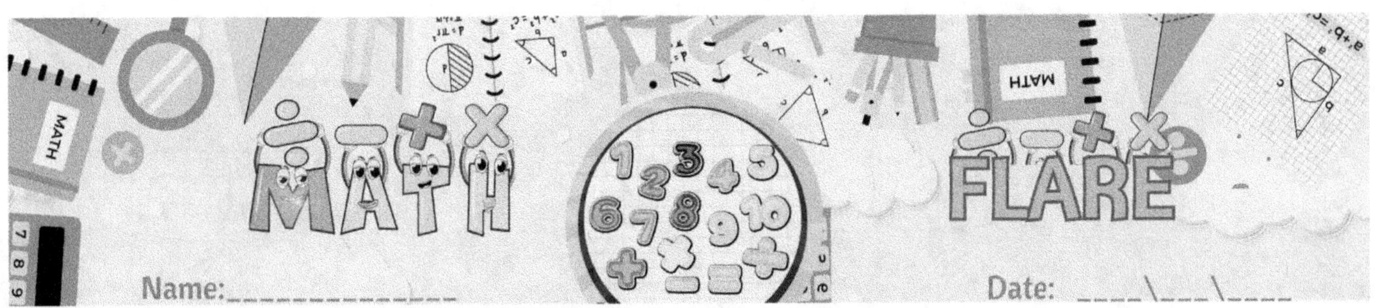

149.

$$8\overline{)52{,}077}$$

150.

$$3\overline{)20{,}134}$$

151.

$$7\overline{)65{,}769}$$

152.

$$8\overline{)97{,}981}$$

153.

$$6\overline{)52{,}094}$$

154.

$$2\overline{)77{,}153}$$

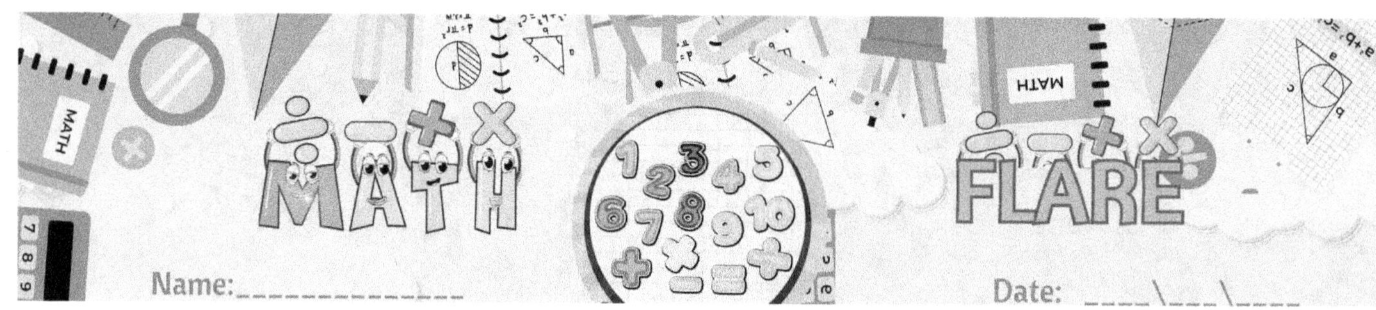

155.

$$17 \overline{)\,53{,}992}$$

156.

$$3 \overline{)\,69{,}371}$$

157.

$$19 \overline{)\,67{,}754}$$

158.

$$17 \overline{)\,77{,}976}$$

159.

$$16 \overline{)\,77{,}642}$$

160.

$$13 \overline{)\,50{,}554}$$

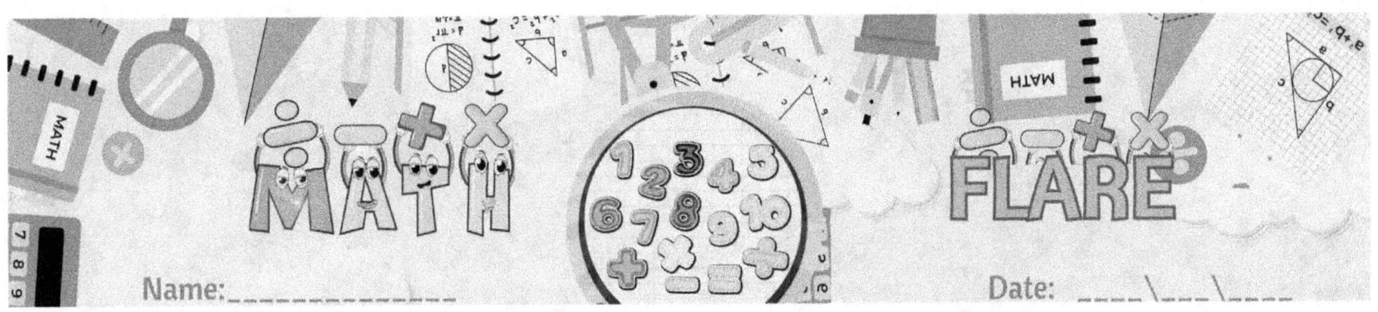

161.

$$19 \overline{)68{,}650}$$

162.

$$16 \overline{)50{,}376}$$

163.

$$5 \overline{)86{,}739}$$

164.

$$15 \overline{)68{,}710}$$

165.

$$20 \overline{)81{,}758}$$

166.

$$5 \overline{)34{,}521}$$

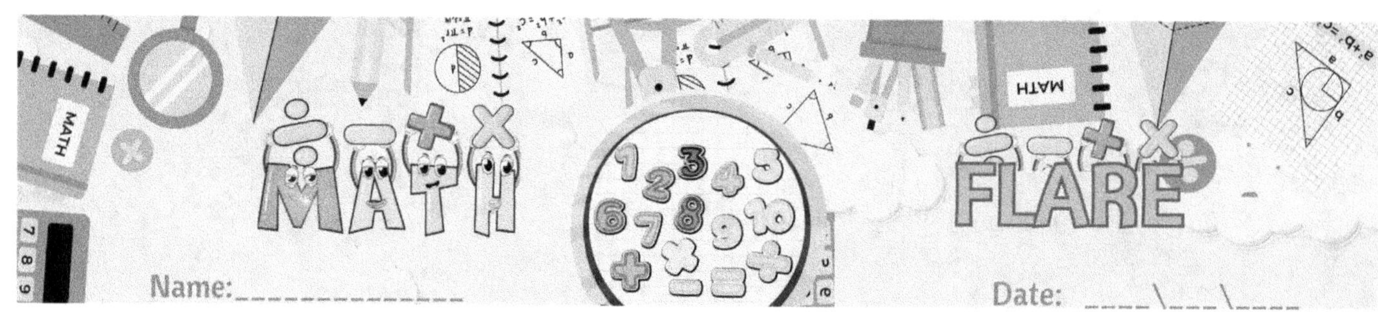

Name: _______________   Date: ____ \ ____ \ ____

167.

$$18 \overline{)\ 49{,}195}$$

168.

$$20 \overline{)\ 76{,}626}$$

169.

$$18 \overline{)\ 54{,}874}$$

170.

$$16 \overline{)\ 24{,}338}$$

171.

$$18 \overline{)\ 87{,}399}$$

172.

$$6 \overline{)\ 70{,}077}$$

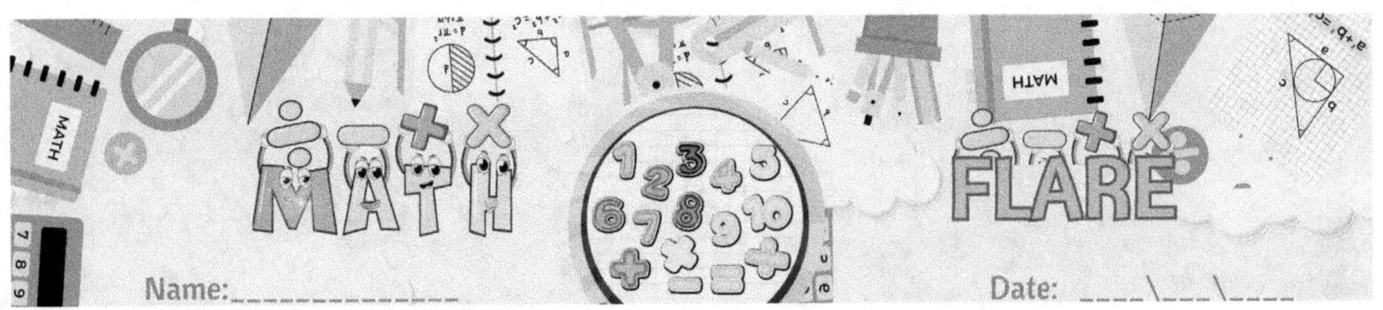

173.

18) 45,806

174.

4) 68,485

175.

3) 29,104

176.

14) 65,259

177.

11) 89,509

178.

14) 45,339

179.

$$5\overline{)86{,}682}$$

180.

$$8\overline{)51{,}649}$$

181.

$$3\overline{)59{,}956}$$

182.

$$11\overline{)28{,}936}$$

183.

$$10\overline{)60{,}830}$$

184.

$$15\overline{)64{,}118}$$

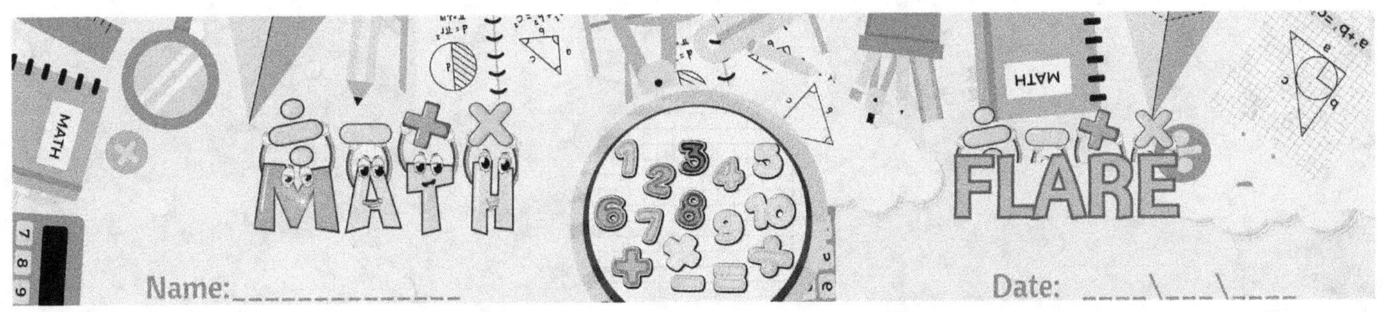

185.

16) 30,140

186.

17) 41,051

187.

14) 65,666

188.

16) 79,263

189.

6) 35,837

190.

20) 46,236

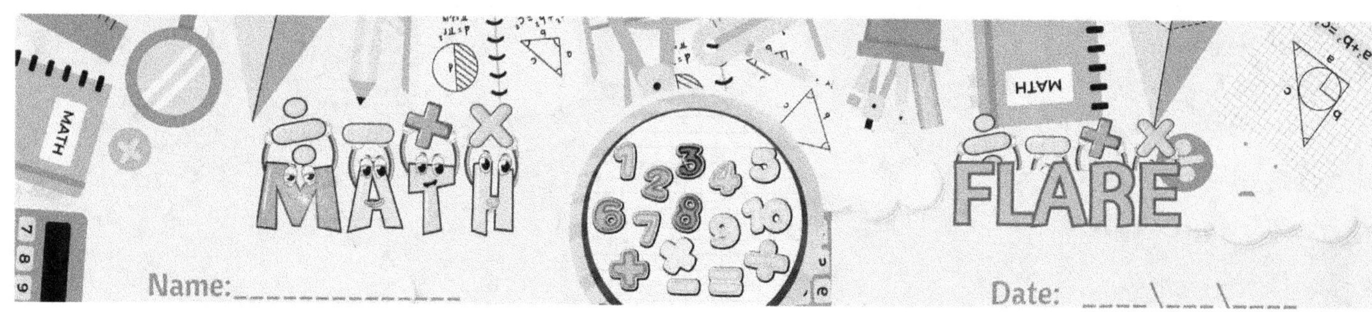

191.

11)̄ 54,717

192.

16)̄ 53,475

193.

12)̄ 42,457

194.

19)̄ 37,433

195.

3)̄ 55,919

196.

8)̄ 23,033

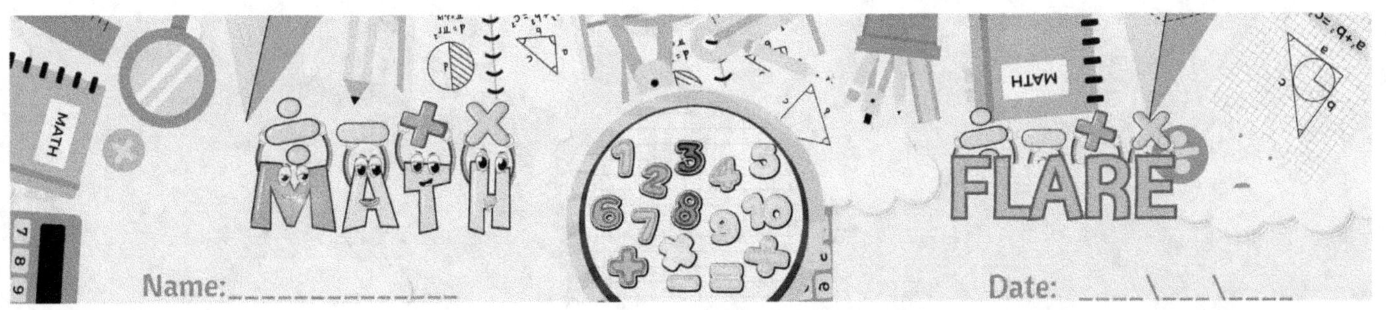

197.

17) 50,019

198.

17) 29,663

199.

5) 69,026

200.

19) 69,644

ANSWERS

Page 1: Long Division

1. 49	2. 18	3. 92	4. 38	5. 65	6. 4	7. 26
8. 87	9. 75	10. 68	11. 16	12. 80	13. 42	14. 50
15. 8	16. 32	17. 99	18. 80	19. 81	20. 29	21. 85
22. 16	23. 28	24. 23	25. 69	26. 14	27. 11	28. 87
29. 57	30. 94	31. 64	32. 80	33. 38	34. 88	35. 39
36. 38	37. 14	38. 18	39. 42	40. 56	41. 57	42. 45
43. 36	44. 75	45. 28	46. 77	47. 72	48. 46	49. 49
50. 24	51. 37	52. 26	53. 17	54. 99	55. 9	56. 3
57. 8	58. 20	59. 65	60. 64	61. 31	62. 61	63. 5
64. 58	65. 88	66. 82	67. 54	68. 66	69. 24	70. 95
71. 24	72. 54	73. 37	74. 5	75. 65	76. 44	77. 31
78. 19	79. 81	80. 4	81. 60	82. 15	83. 58	84. 83
85. 9	86. 64	87. 98	88. 19	89. 4	90. 53	91. 63
92. 83	93. 22	94. 47	95. 43	96. 56	97. 36	98. 47
99. 66	100. 48	101. 25	102. 66	103. 92	104. 39	105. 52
106. 67	107. 91	108. 79	109. 7	110. 13	111. 59	112. 20
113. 82	114. 74	115. 60	116. 37	117. 28	118. 77	119. 61
120. 46	121. 97	122. 59	123. 86	124. 41	125. 51	126. 33
127. 64	128. 40	129. 50	130. 99	131. 5	132. 50	133. 99

134. 92	135. 26	136. 47	137. 22	138. 49	139. 9	140. 30
141. 64	142. 21	143. 55	144. 97	145. 1	146. 33	147. 12
148. 19	149. 92	150. 48	151. 14	152. 27	153. 14	154. 6
155. 62	156. 15	157. 74	158. 87	159. 48	160. 31	161. 32
162. 48	163. 73	164. 65	165. 49	166. 75	167. 35	168. 3
169. 86	170. 7	171. 94	172. 90	173. 71	174. 64	175. 38
176. 87	177. 12	178. 58	179. 75	180. 30	181. 53	182. 91
183. 68	184. 68	185. 8	186. 98	187. 29	188. 35	189. 93
190. 8	191. 83	192. 58	193. 92	194. 74	195. 78	196. 55
197. 50	198. 55	199. 49	200. 43			

Page 14: Long Division

1. 237	2. 812	3. 741	4. 558	5. 92	6. 666	7. 707
8. 694	9. 62	10. 84	11. 486	12. 855	13. 489	14. 75
15. 876	16. 458	17. 830	18. 894	19. 118	20. 38	21. 22
22. 681	23. 738	24. 710	25. 216	26. 336	27. 930	28. 136
29. 621	30. 55	31. 113	32. 997	33. 131	34. 821	35. 645
36. 627	37. 252	38. 473	39. 524	40. 137	41. 215	42. 800
43. 342	44. 878	45. 822	46. 936	47. 322	48. 434	49. 893
50. 62	51. 68	52. 306	53. 174	54. 943	55. 455	56. 507
57. 800	58. 603	59. 740	60. 73	61. 977	62. 925	63. 201
64. 364	65. 103	66. 699	67. 603	68. 533	69. 816	70. 902

71. 318   72. 447   73. 357   74. 379   75. 616   76. 739   77. 196

78. 903   79. 36   80. 877   81. 286   82. 291   83. 841   84. 354

85. 921   86. 174   87. 20   88. 550   89. 472   90. 425   91. 70

92. 416   93. 254   94. 352   95. 219   96. 844   97. 406   98. 195

99. 441   100. 625   101. 945   102. 272   103. 953   104. 642   105. 677

106. 100   107. 657   108. 497   109. 210   110. 189   111. 195   112. 132

113. 174   114. 974   115. 298   116. 204   117. 596   118. 551   119. 387

120. 773

Page 28:   Long Division: Remainders

1. 2,014 R8   2. 6,310 R1   3. 16,901 R4   4. 2,450 R5

5. 3,639 R12   6. 3,784 R8   7. 2,070 R6   8. 5,488 R2

9. 11,679 R3   10. 3,764 R1   11. 1,182 R10   12. 13,689 R3

13. 5,425 R2   14. 26,752 R1   15. 7,982 R4   16. 6,885 R4

17. 8,876 R1   18. 18,953 R1   19. 1,932 R3   20. 2,666 R8

21. 12,329 R2   22. 7,035 R1   23. 5,084 R5   24. 9,889 R4

25. 7,099 R10   26. 11,456 R0   27. 4,980 R9   28. 7,721 R0

29. 2,024 R5   30. 4,035 R0   31. 11,775 R0   32. 2,104 R0

33. 7,558 R2   34. 940 R17   35. 8,891 R1   36. 3,719 R3

37. 5,654 R1   38. 3,797 R9   39. 7,628 R6   40. 3,992 R10

41. 4,201 R7   42. 1,361 R10   43. 2,312 R3   44. 2,172 R6

45. 5,937 R3   46. 9,136 R0   47. 2,736 R1   48. 2,049 R7

49. 1,500 R7   50. 7,079 R9   51. 3,622 R1   52. 5,369 R3

53. 2,428 R9   54. 3,783 R2   55. 2,648 R1   56. 46,612 R1

57. 16,852 R2   58. 13,296 R1   59. 14,052 R6   60. 5,938 R2

61. 1,754 R2   62. 3,736 R1   63. 3,380 R0   64. 6,727 R0

65. 3,227 R2   66. 5,561 R0   67. 3,300 R1   68. 9,769 R1

69. 6,387 R9   70. 5,416 R0   71. 1,239 R13   72. 2,054 R16

73. 3,606 R14   74. 13,973 R5   75. 6,626 R0   76. 4,671 R5

77. 7,246 R7   78. 7,021 R5   79. 3,152 R13   80. 11,786 R2

81. 18,676 R1   82. 5,864 R13   83. 3,715 R7   84. 4,383 R5

85. 1,414 R3   86. 2,859 R1   87. 4,363 R6   88. 4,225 R1

89. 1,936 R5   90. 5,649 R6   91. 4,921 R19   92. 17,085 R3

93. 6,529 R4   94. 20,711 R0   95. 4,563 R9   96. 4,439 R14

97. 11,739 R5   98. 7,543 R3   99. 1,520 R1   100. 11,155 R4

101. 4,749 R1   102. 2,165 R5   103. 1,902 R7   104. 1,862 R16

105. 6,209 R6   106. 4,422 R0   107. 5,981 R3   108. 4,306 R2

109. 1,848 R7   110. 6,367 R9   111. 9,296 R5   112. 8,241 R2

113. 4,533 R0   114. 4,755 R1   115. 3,049 R14   116. 945 R10

117. 7,046 R9   118. 2,867 R3   119. 8,921 R8   120. 1,968 R5

121. 2,254 R13   122. 9,859 R6   123. 4,084 R12   124. 4,896 R3

125. 981 R13   126. 10,708 R4   127. 4,220 R16   128. 12,386 R1

129. 4,817 R5   130. 13,051 R1   131. 1,938 R13   132. 4,642 R0

133. 2,837 R10   134. 1,815 R10   135. 5,450 R2   136. 3,089 R11

137. 4,974 R5   138. 2,707 R4   139. 4,749 R11   140. 11,903 R6

141. 3,342 R3   142. 2,311 R6   143. 7,559 R2   144. 17,727 R4

145. 5,272 R2   146. 13,220 R1   147. 1,000 R16   148. 9,923 R4

149. 6,509 R5   150. 6,711 R1   151. 9,395 R4   152. 12,247 R5

153. 8,682 R2   154. 38,576 R1   155. 3,176 R0   156. 23,123 R2

157. 3,566 R0   158. 4,586 R14   159. 4,852 R10   160. 3,888 R10

161. 3,613 R3   162. 3,148 R8   163. 17,347 R4   164. 4,580 R10

165. 4,087 R18   166. 6,904 R1   167. 2,733 R1   168. 3,831 R6

169. 3,048 R10   170. 1,521 R2   171. 4,855 R9   172. 11,679 R3

173. 2,544 R14   174. 17,121 R1   175. 9,701 R1   176. 4,661 R5

177. 8,137 R2   178. 3,238 R7   179. 17,336 R2   180. 6,456 R1

181. 19,985 R1   182. 2,630 R6   183. 6,083 R0   184. 4,274 R8

185. 1,883 R12   186. 2,414 R13   187. 4,690 R6   188. 4,953 R15

189. 5,972 R5   190. 2,311 R16   191. 4,974 R3   192. 3,342 R3

193. 3,538 R1   194. 1,970 R3   195. 18,639 R2   196. 2,879 R1

197. 2,942 R5   198. 1,744 R15   199. 13,805 R1   200. 3,665 R9